The Last Horn

*Someone screamed stat. "Give me the cardio-epi or this show is over. Get off those Ski-boots so I can see the toes. We need a full set of cranial scans **yesterday**. How long was the flight off the mountain? Vitals are scary, can we get an EEG asap. If we don't see brainwave activity we'll need some authorization to continue life-support."* Calm and warm it seems like an audience of one for hospital dinner theatre. A luminescent tunnel beckons me onward. I feel as though I could travel through time and space. The tension below doesn't affect me as I don't feel attached to that scene anymore. I drift without moving… *"He's crashing charge the paddles and ready, clear…bang, once again ready, clear, bang"*

Pushing with each ski in a skating maneuver to gain quick acceleration I head down the deserted slope and accelerate rapidly. I crouch into a tuck position with elbows at my sides and knees pressed to my chest, and skis eighteen inches apart, thus creating the most aerodynamic profile for the assault down the mountain. I head into the first long roundhouse turn which can be managed without sacrificing any speed and staying compressed in order to maintain maximum speed heading into the steep sidewinder ahead. The roar of the wind is intense, and the chattering of the skis edges as they hold the suddenly icy slope and a large rooster tail of shredded snow follows me like a shadow as I descend further down the mountain. My thighs are starting to burn as fatigue sets in, and a certain rubbery feel to the legs permeates my thoughts, but I must remove these thoughts from my mind as any deviance from total concentration at this point will spell ruin. As the crest of the next ridge approaches I know the steepest is yet to come, as I have covered these slopes for countless runs in the past. The wind is screaming as I descend further and the slope nears a more vertical profile, and I accelerate even more with heart pounding and legs burning. I do not surrender to the discomfort and forge further down the mountain towards what has been nicknamed the camel bumps. The trick to the camels is to pre-jump the first in the series and take a little distance from the second without too much height, because if you do not address the camels correctly they will devastate you by causing spectacular crashes. I take a little hop over the first camel and jump the second sailing thirty meters in the air, but only a few feet off the ground and land gently tuck position intact.

Two hundred pairs of eyes directed at me with the utmost vehemence and absolute hatred, it would have been more easy to bear if there were a seat at the front of the bus, but these assembled teachers and students had been waiting an hour and a half in a somewhat diesel-choked bus, and had become very angry with the cause of their delay, whose death march to the back of the bus seemed to take an eternity. Not a word was spoken and none were necessary as the eyes of the gathered pierced me with messages of extreme loathing. A light layer of snow was falling which would require chains on a public vehicle adding another forty-five minutes to a return trip that would already be an eternity, because of the cloud of repugnance in the air.

When the Claxon sounds the mountain is closed. The sharp bark of the Claxon horn can pierce the mountain air and be heard for miles and those on the slopes should be aware that the chairs will stop running and the ski patrol will wait a compulsory twenty minutes and sweep down the mountain looking for stragglers. This routine occurred at five pm or dusk depending which happened first. To wait for the patrol to pass and have the trail to one's self was the ultimate goal. To blaze down a pre-chosen path as though it were a downhill course and carry as much speed as possible all the way to the bottom, finishing with a snow spewing final flourishing skidding stop.

More than halfway down the mountain and still accelerating, always looking for the fastest line of descent, I continue the run despite the growing pain in my legs. One or two luge-like turns and I will be heading towards a straight-line finish. I power into the last series of turns holding position and riding high into the bank of the turn, I catch an edge briefly and set the ski back down gently as to make no sudden moves at this speed. I enter the last turn if I can hold form here I can make it without a serious crash, and at speed approaching forty-five miles an hour crashes are to be avoided at all costs.

Badger Pass in Yosemite National Park was a short bus ride from Clovis California and once in a while a destination for Junior High Field trips. This was the case in the winter of seventy-three. A group was assembled at a pre-selected parking lot and a precursory role was taken and the generic Greyhound took off for the Sierra Mountains. With a large group there are typical songs to be sung and adolescent hijinks to be performed, but generally speaking the two and a half hour bus ride was uneventful. The same trip up the mountain could be accomplished in two hours or less depending on who was driving. There was also no ice chest to snack from as was the routine in a family car and other differences would become apparent later that day.

We grabbed our skis and other equipment and rushed off for the lift line. In the mad dash from the diesel choked parking lot to the more pristine lodge and chairlift areas there had been some semblance of rules, procedures and other directions from our illustrious teacher chaperones that were somewhat ignored by the excited teens. One of which to be found out later was an imposed curfew of three-thirty sharp, to meet back at the bus equipment et all. Typically at fifteen years old one does not cherish time spent in the realm of nature's beauty, instead the tribe of Nordic sportsmen would ski as fast as possible and try to accumulate as many runs down the mountain as possible, even skipping lunch if that were imaginable for teenagers. The skill level was diverse amongst this group. Some were skiing fast and falling a lot and could be described as tumbling down the mountain and skiing a little in between tumbling runs, while others could only manage to be upright for a brief few seconds at a time. These skill differences created a separation from classmates and those who could ski fast and error free were soon not among their Nordic compatriots for the duration.

As the apex of the turn approaches I am feeling elated and fatigued at the same time. The pain of exertion in my legs has turned to numbness, and even the cold mountain air is burning my lungs as the run comes to a close. I am trying to hold my line through the turn as the suddenly much icier conditions are becoming treacherous. My skis are bouncing instead of holding the line firmly and my stamina seems to be disintegrating as the conditions worsen. It is becoming almost dark and the bumps are much harder to see in the mountain twilight, this can cause mistakes, and the icy snow is much like concrete as far as forgiveness goes. Time seems to have slowed as I am holding my line through the turn, it feels as though the action is slow motion, but the sound of the wind screeching and my heart thumping like a disco kick drum are in real time. I exit the turn and continue with the bumps, which are now virtually unseen, bouncing me up and down precariously as my skis track towards the finish.

Splashdown

It was like being caught in the bottom of a waterfall with a tumbling of bodies and continual motion that was unpredictable, savage yet controlled. The exertion factor was at a premium. Where the action was taking place the water looked like a maelstrom of micro rainbows and arced splashes, and yet there were patches of open water, still and shinning like glass. From a distance the pool looked as though a pod of dolphins were having a rumble with their rivals. It was sunny for a winter's day and the habitual morning fog had long since departed. When the first whistles were blown the weather was perfect for the action at hand. The first whistle began a dual sprint opposing players start from opposite ends, and the ball is placed in the middle of the pool. If you dig very hard with every stroke and kick like

Neptune is chasing you, the ball can be won and possession achieved. That being accomplished we score rather quickly after a series of quick passes. When competing against an overmatched opponent there is a tendency to play down or subconsciously commit uncharacteristic errors. If you let them think they are in the game, then to some degree they are. This contest between highly ranked and unranked does not proceed as expected and what should have been a scrimmage like atmosphere becomes a desperate struggle of leviathan-like proportions. The score is close enough to still pull out a victory albeit an embarrassing one. Cinch down the defense and create some turnovers and with superior speed and agility this contest will be over. Sometimes in the course of an athletic endeavor the internal dialogue can slow down as oxygen debt is approached, where the seven seconds it takes to cover twenty meters in a pool can seem like minutes or even hours in extreme situations.

This was one of those periods of time that lasts longer than it should and dwelled in memory even longer. Playing very tight defense in the closing moments would yield a turnover and the time was ripe to take off like a trophy fish that will not be caught. Taking a little poetic license with a push off the hip, because an obvious push from the chest will result in an offensive foul we cannot have at this juncture. Number three is out on the break churning water as though there is a tow rope underwater; being caught is not a reality. Too much speed and distance for the possibility of being overtaken, though someone always trails in hopes of the unthinkable, unforeseen happenstance. Athletes at this level do not run out of gas, swimming fifteen to twenty thousand meters a day will insure that.

Time has now slowed almost to a dead stop. The sounds and cheering and yelling have become a whale's baseline with no discernible breaks. Taking a look backwards for the sight of the ball arcing downward ever so slowly, but accurate as though guided by a laser it lands a few feet in front of the chin, but not so far away for a goalie to come out from his cage and intercept it. Breakaways are the stuff that makes practicing for games entertaining; it becomes second nature after thousands of repetitions. As the goalmouth approaches one will juke to one side and more than likely shoot to the other, providing the goalie has not already committed to one side or the other. These scenarios and probabilities have been addressed countless times and drilled out of the realm of reaction rather than deduction. The long hours it seemingly took to swim twenty meters has elapsed and the ball already having arrived it is time to deliver it to its destination and end this troublesome foray. With a quick shift from right hand to left hand, and drill the rock out of this dimension, to propel the ball with the utmost velocity in a predestined visualized target location within the goal. With all the force of a Faulkner phrase the ball hits the crossbar and rebounds harmlessly away, with no chance for a rapid second shot. The clock runs out and Portland State has a moral victory with a tie.

The pool at this end has a sixteen foot depth, and there are observation windows for those curious souls that yearn to know what actually happens underwater. Swimming down to the bottom is a temporary evasion; alas the windows do not open like submarine hatches.

The stench of a grievous error is discernible even at this depth. If one could obtain some diving gear perhaps one could remain in this underwater shelter till the players have left and the crowd dispersed. Or even sneak out to an unfamiliar dining hall and then trek up into the high Sierras till the unthinkable is forgotten. If your psyche is torn asunder, how long will it take to heal? The cranial burn is very intense. The vivid and intensely painful recollection of this recent error is an example of the human ability to punish itself. The wrath of the internal dialogue can be merciless by repeating an event within the mind over and over like an overzealous video tape editor with a penchant for repetition, reliving the capsule in a timeless loop always wishing for another outcome that never transpires. Sometimes a herculean effort of a physical nature will provide temporary relief, such as five sets of forty handstand pushups, which had been a frequent remedy for the author and subject of this recollection. A weekend or even a month or two, it might even take thirty years to forgive oneself for an event that has only the value to which one gives it. Stockton, California and the University of the Pacific are thousands of miles away now, but the memories that were etched in the mind there are never very far away.

Leaf Blower Nation

As a landscaper employs a leaf blower to blow the leaves from an assigned area and never picks them up, to a nation that fixes problems by moving monies or assets to another area is avoiding the root problem. The mess simply moves to another area, as unfortunately our government seems to move assets or bail out conglomerates while we have people losing their homes and children going hungry. While the bailout money is used to fund corporate retreats and incentive bonuses for executives, the plight of middle America is accentuated by this sweep it under the carpet mentality. Financial problems that are not solved by finding the source of the difficulty are doomed to continue until the root issue is resolved.

Just as anyone would push a pile from one side of the desk to the other America has continued a path of avoidance especially in regards to finance. The core difficulty of our national economy is that it is built on speculation. Just as any house or structure that is built on a faulty foundation is doomed to collapse, the same has happened to our economy. Until we fix the problem at the source we will experience repeated events of insolvency. The Fed has repeatedly bailed out banks and other financial entities that are deemed too big to fail. Referring to the bailout as economic stabilization gives the American people a new term that has a friendlier connotation, and will placate the general public with a more acceptable term for something they would otherwise be outraged. It is not unusual for government to designate policies or events to make them more readily digestible, such as referring to war as a police action or torture as enhanced interrogation.

An economy built on speculation as ours is can be unstable. The whims of a few investors can set the trend of a mass selloff that will send the industrial averages spiraling towards yet another recession. Selloffs can lead to recession and recession can lead to depression, which will cause large banks to fail and bailouts will occur. Bailouts will be termed "economic stabilizations" to soften the grievous financial jurisprudence. The total of bailout funds ends up being a very large sum of money and it has to come from somewhere. The American taxpayers are footing the bill for large corporate bailouts, the same middle class American taxpayers on the verge of losing their homes and possessions without any chance of a bailout. The people who do not have enough to eat are paying for the corporate retreats some of these board of directors have given themselves with the hard-earned dollars the Fed gave them to keep their proverbial ships afloat. The really awful thing about this scenario is the greater percentage of the population does not know who paid for the mess to be cleaned up, and how it can affect them in the future. John Q. Citizen paid for Big Bank to stay afloat and with the trickle-down effect John Q. will continue to pay in irregular installments.

The latent effect for the Middle American consumer is when recession hits, the basic essential commodities that bolster our existence become more expensive and some unaffordable. Healthcare has to be considered a luxury in some homes, and with food costs escalating at an exorbitant rate many households are cutting back on fresher healthier items because they simply cannot afford them. Unfortunately for the American people they cannot elect someone who can fix these problems in one term. The probability of economic recovery in less than ten years is remote at best. An overhaul of our financial structure is required and the present government in place is not moving in that direction and not likely to be any time soon.

The super Pac backing that puts our leaders in office will not allow such changes to take place. As long as elected officials depend on campaign contributions to get them in office the public is doomed to walk the same path for as long as it takes to amend the election process. Until the election process has been rectified the financial changes, which are necessary to bring America back to some semblance of financial global leadership, will not occur.

The Government enforced no requirements on banks for dispersement of cash. The financial stipulations written into the original document, but later revisions were added because the banks threatened not to accept the money (Taibbi). Monies that had been originally earmarked for home lending and small business the Government reduced from their original intent to an insignificant amount. In theory the billions had been intended to help Middle America, but after a great deal of political maneuvering the end result was that big banks became bigger and if they had once been considered too big to fail, they became even bigger and created a more substantial safety net for themselves. The proverbial candy dish offered by big government and intended for homeowners and small business was snatched away by a bully of enormous size and financial hunger. Had the original restrictions been adhered to, this probably would not have taken place or at the very least not to the extent that occurred. Furthermore, if systems are in place and they are ineffective and or not enforced, what recourse do the American people have at this point, can the courts become involved after the fact to undo any financial injustices that need rectifying? If the American people were swindled out of seven hundred billion dollars that some percentage of which should have been distributed to the aid of small business and home lending, would the possibility exist that someone could say we want our money back, and if so could there be a reasonable course to retrieve said funds and reroute them to their original intended destination?

As rivers that flow into the sea become salt water, funds that become intertwined with big business grow tainted to the extent that they can never be fully recovered or returned to their pristine mountain stream state. With exploration of how bailout funds were dispersed and the discovery of certain irregularities therein attained, it would be reasonable to commence a recovery effort to reclaim monies from bonuses and corporate retreats in violation of the original bailout stipulations. Even if a small percentage was recovered it could be used to save a home or feed a child who might otherwise go hungry.

Turning back the clock has never been a viable option for financial misdeeds; as a gambler would relate, once the bet is lost it is gone forever. This has not been the case for large banks and other financial conglomerates. They have been given a third free throw, a fourth strike or a mythical second chance after overextending themselves and ill-advised lending. They gambled and lost, yet are given a second and more than likely third chance to speculate yet again. This would be acceptable if big business was playing the game with their money, contrary to John Q. Homeowner who if he were to gamble on a not so affordable mortgage and lose his job, there will be no Fed or any other financial entity to step in and pay off an ill-advised mortgage. If the average citizen revises his retirement stock portfolio to include higher risk and larger gain investments and loses his retirement, he will simply have to continue working.

    The fact that our economy is built on speculation is the prime factor of our financial dilemmas. Factoring the loss of funds through too many layers of bureaucracy and simple mismanagement, our financial backbone has been systematically gambled away to the extent that financial recovery is seemingly impossible. Speculation in moderation is an acceptable form of financial gain. However, if speculation is the primary form of profit or as in the American case the cornerstone of our financial system, changes need to occur and rapidly in order to ensure some form of financial security for the future. As profits become harder to attain the more the tendency to speculate is utilized by corporate America. The desire for quick solutions is understandable, but the obvious pitfall of the nation when funds that do not really exist are gambled and lost. A gambler's thoughts are often described as innocuous musings and rationalizations to commence a dominance of the internal dialogue regarding when to quit and the irrepressible one more roll to recoup losses. National addiction to gambling is at an all-time high, and that is without factoring in speculative behaviors such as the stock market and short-sale real estate. It is no big mystery that our populace at all economic levels participates in games of chance, whether financial or otherwise. These behaviors manifest in a desire to attain wealth quickly. Sometimes that desire is born out of desperation because of debt, and sometimes originating from the inability to procure a level of financial comfort in reference to savings and retirement. The speculative nature of our national economy has a trickle-down effect from the Wall Street boardrooms to the living rooms of Middle America, where each entity will bet more than can be reasonably lost in an effort to better their respective financial situations. The main difference between the two being an errant boardroom decision that precludes billion dollar losses has a good chance of being underwritten by the Fed, because that boardroom entity is considered too big to fail.

The deceptive nature of those involved in the procuring and spending of the bailout funds cannot necessarily be deemed criminal, but the audacity in which it was achieved goes beyond measure. The original proposals for small business written into the verbiage to pacify doubters and essentially to sell the proposals to Congress were readily disposed of, not being deleted just simply ignored. So the good faith and intention that was the inspiration of the Home Affordable Modification Program (HAMP) act and its successors were subsequently purged from the active applications of the bailout and not to be mentioned again until more funds were sought. When original bailout proposals were being drafted there were objections by some that if there were too many restrictions the banks would not participate (Taibbi1). This could have been a turning point in this financial debacle, because financial institutions would not accept government money because of too many restrictions, then let the game continue without them, and provide the bailout money to those who are willing to participate within the prescribed guidelines. A wake up call was missed at that juncture, for if the same banks that would not participate because of conditions were more than likely the same who dealt out bonuses and funds for corporate retreats. Creating incendiary reaction by public and media in regards to the cavalier attitude in which the public funds being dispersed. This would not preface enlightenment that the authors or the first bailout would be once burned and twice warned. In the subsequent bailout maneuvers the recipients of federal funds used what was intended for economic simulation to pay off their previous TARP loans and what turned out to be a reduced interest rate. The American taxpayers were duped again, although indirectly as they were represented by the Fed and Congress. If financial conglomerates were subject to the same scrutiny and stipulations that a homeowner would have to face in initiating a new loan, one would find a great deal less irregularity in their financial behavior.

Legalities aside, the corporate bailout proved a travesty to the sanctity of American Jurisprudence, since the regulators assigned to oversee the giant nest egg were out sleuthed by the media. If overzealous media personnel did not actively investigate the whole TARP fiasco it's highly possible that a great deal of the improprieties that occurred would have gone unnoticed by the actual government personnel assigned to the task. If the federal government were left to its own devices many financial misdeeds would be swept under the carpet or better described as blown away from the immediate area as the landscaper's helper blows leaves from one yard to another.

It is criminal to allow funds to be diverted from their intended destination, to be invested in an ill-advised manner, and one must tread a fine line to follow the cash trail and then determine if legalities are infringed upon. Intent is a hard thing to prove and if the subject is a well-informed financial professional the burden of proof becomes even more taxing. It is an honorable thing to catch and prosecute individuals that tamper with enormous sums of cash, although once accomplished the cash is rarely recovered. Even if a conviction was attained it accomplishes little for the people that suffer the most, which are the lower income citizens who least could afford financial difficulties. It seems as though good intention by the president and Congress was thwarted by corporate moguls whose thirst for profits has driven them to erroneous investments that result in financial hard times for everyone but themselves.

When the large conglomerates fail the government will have to pay, regardless of whether a bailout occurs or have to subsidize thousands of workers who are suddenly without sustenance. The point of concern is whether the amount of cash can be monitored and directed to those who would most require the assistance. Essentially it would be ideal to have what human nature dictates, the innate behavior of helping beings in distress to be directed to feed the hungry not overload the coffers of the fabulously wealthy.

Confidence lost would be an accurate description of the bailout and its aftermath as the American people try to dig themselves out of a financial pit that was created when Congress allowed seven-hundred billion dollars to be entrusted to unscrupulous financial entities that did not use their windfall as prescribed.

Exhaustive research has revealed financial ramifications of not only the bailout of corporate America, but also the core problems that led to the downfall of some of our largest and seemingly indestructible financial institutions. The leanings of our government, however noble in their original ideas, are to fix problems in an easy manner rather than solve issues from their core which would be the most beneficial for the future. The continuance of these financial problem solving philosophies will only add to their complexity and also the longevity of their existence. If some semblance of restraint is achieved and a more critical thinking approach is adopted towards these financial endeavors there could be a chance for economic recovery. Leadership on all levels would have to work in unison to achieve financial recovery, as the political infighting is counterproductive to the process. The foibles of corporate America parallel a gardener blowing a mess of leaves to another yard rather than picking them up and mulching them, or at the very least just picking up the mess and moving on.

Work Consulted

Bernanke, Ben S. "A Cautiously Optimistic Economic Forecast." Vital Speeches Of The Day 76.1 (2010): 32-36. Academic Search Complete. Web. 11 Mar. 2013.

Bernanke, Ben S. "Bank Supervision In The United States." Vital Speeches Of The Day 73.2 (2007): 61. MAS Ultra - School Edition. Web. 11 Mar. 2013.

Bernanke, Chairman Ben S. "Flexibility And Optimism In An Unpredictable World." *Boston College Law Review* 50.(2009): 941. LexisNexis Academic: Law Reviews. Web. 11 Mar. 2013.

Fabian, Nelson. "MANAGING EDITOR's DESK. World Rankings Of The U.S. ... Education ... NEHA." *Journal Of Environmental Health* 73.7 (2011): 58-38. *Academic Search Complete*. Web. 7 Mar. 2013.

Heike, Jöns, and Hoyler Michael. "Global Geographies Of Higher Education: The Perspective Of World University Rankings." *Geoforum* (n.d.): *ScienceDirect*. Web. 7 Mar. 2013.

Kuhl, Lester. "maintaining a nation's middle class in the global economy: a systems engineering analysis of the american economic system and the middle class." *world future review* 4.2 (2012): 83-95. *academic search complete*. web. 7 mar. 2013.

Siskey, Kyle, and Elizabeth Fournier. "How The Bailouts Should Change Regulation." *International Financial Law Review* 27.11 (2008): 20-24. Business Source Complete. Web. 10 Mar. 2013.

Taibbi, Matt. "Secrets And Lies Of The Bailout." Rolling Stone 1174 (2013): 34. MasterFILE Premier. Web. 16 Mar. 2013.

The Texas Decriminalization of Marijuana

Texas should pass legislation for the legalization of medical Marijuana. This legislation should accomplish several things. First the legalization of Medical Marijuana in Texas (lMMT) should provide increased tax revenue for the state government to help with budget constraints. Secondly the (lMMT) would help law enforcement with a reduction in drug violence statewide. Thirdly the (lMMT) would provide symptomatic relief to cancer and Aids patients who suffer from ailments that are relieved by medical Marijuana. Finally the (lMMT) would cause a de-valuation of Marijuana, and that will make it a less desirable product for illegal importers and organized crime syndicates.

This type of legislation has already been tried in several other states, including California, Colorado, and Alaska. It must be noted that the Federal government has made no concessions to the medical use of Marijuana and still considers it illegal. The technical legality between Federal and State governments presents a difficult situation for respective law enforcement agencies. Bostwick tell us "As an increasing number of states legalize marijuana's medical use, the federal government maintains its resolute stance that its use for any reason is criminal, a stance that renders prescribers simultaneously law-abiding healers and defiant scofflaws. (172)" State officials must adhere to State laws as written, and at any given time their policies can be over ridden by Federal officials. "Despite marijuana's current classification as a Schedule I agent under the federal Controlled Substances Act, a designation declaring it to have high abuse potential and no currently accepted medical use, physicians and the general public alike are in broad agreement that Cannabis sativa shows promise in combating diverse medical ills" (Bostwick 172). While States are allowing Botanical growers to produce Medical Marijuana, it is only at this point being allowed to continue while the Federal government turns a blind eye in that direction. The definition of Botanical growers in reference to Medical Marijuana is varied from state to state, but the essence is growers who produce medical Marijuana in a greenhouse environment and under strict control as far as the counting and registering of the plants on an each basis. This system creates an inventory control factor and the whereabouts of the product can be monitored to eliminate theft and misappropriation.

The decriminalization of Marijuana can be mitigating factor in the war on drugs. As the law enforcement officials can concentrate more on hard drugs such as heroin and methamphetamine which are more destructive to society and very addictive. The production of methamphetamine and heroin have increased in the U.S. over the last decade these type of addictive drugs have an effect that produces an increase in theft and robberies because the addicts will go to great lengths to procure their drugs. With more man-hours to work with because the police are not concentrating on Marijuana law enforcement and can be redistributed to eradicate hard drug crime.

"Nonetheless, many believe a lot less blood would be shed if America were to legalize pot, which according to some estimates accounts for 60 percent of Mexico's drug trade with the U.S., in much the same way that ending Prohibition in 1933 cut short the careers of tommy-gun-wielding gangsters. "(Conant, Eve et all 1) Legislation cannot generally eliminate crime, however if it can reduce drug related homicides it would certainly be worthwhile.

    The concentration factor of medical Marijuana has thus far not been addressed in any current legislation. The concentration being the percentage of tetrahydrocannabinol (THC) present in the harvested form of the marijuana plant. This concentration affects the medicinal potency of marijuana as well as a contributing factor of the cash value of the crop.

Bostwick from the Mayo clinic tells us "Anyone with a credit card has ready access to blueprints for marijuana propagation and culture. The concentration of -9-tetrahydrocannabinol (THC), the psychoactive ingredient in cannabis, ranges from less than 0.2% in fiber-type hemp (so-called ditch weed) to 30% in the flower buds of highly hybridized sinsemilla." (173) this high percentage of THC is what botanical growers strive for in their pursuit of a higher grade product.

For the patient or consumer the larger percentage of THC will mean a smaller dosage, but the smaller dosage will also mean a more costly prescription. As de-valuation of botanical Marijuana will occur from the legalization of medical Marijuana the prescription price will drop and unfortunately so will the profit for the grower." The fact is that many small time growers are paying their mortgage and feeding their families from profits on illegal marijuana. Nobody is going to vote to reduce the price of weed from $300/oz to $60/oz when that takes food out of their kids' mouths. (Vlahos, Kelley Beaucar 18) If law makers are looking to reduce the amount of Marijuana grown in the States they should consider legislation that will ultimately de-value the product and therefore disillusion the growers that produce the product.

However from the standpoint of what the state of Texas should do about this problem, it should be noted that the presence of drug markets in border areas, particularly in Juarez, and Brownsville have demonstrated a very abnormal murder rate. ", according to the FBI, more than 1,600 people were killed by cartel violence in Juárez. El Paso, a city of 755,000, recorded just 18 murders in the same year. Laredo had 11 (del Bosque, Melissa)" Quite simply if the emergence of Marijuana legislation could reduce the drug violence in the previously stated areas it certainly be worthwhile to proceed with the necessary litigation to implement these laws concerning botanical Marijuana in a timely fashion. What makes the drug trade attractive to organized crime is the high profit margin. If the profit margin were to be reduced and the involvement of organized crime factions along with it, the overall crime rates would be diminished accordingly. These factors alone would make the Marijuana legislation a worthwhile endeavor.

The prohibition description has been applied to Marijuana initiatives as an indication that laws do not necessarily prevent consumption of an illicit substance, but it has proven to be an enticement for organized crime to become involved in the process. The American consumption of Marijuana has been a motivating factor to those individuals that cultivate and smuggle Marijuana."How does one win a drug war when millions of Americans who use recreational drugs are financing the cartels bribing, murdering, and beheading to win the war and keep self-indulgent Americans supplied with drugs?"(Conant, Eve, and Katie Maloney 1) If a large percentage of people are habitually using an illicit substance and the existing laws are not a deterrent, then the law as it stands is not having the desired effect. The existing Marijuana laws are not preventing the use of the drug, but creating criminals of individuals who would otherwise not be considered criminal. These laws are not designed to create criminals, but rather to prevent the consumption of controlled substances and prevent their distribution and sales.

One of the big problems legislators have with Marijuana is their theory that it is a stepping stone to more dangerous and addictive drugs. That ultimately the use of Marijuana will influence individuals to try other drugs such as Heroin, Cocaine, and Methamphetamine. This progression has certainly occurred, however there is no conclusive evidence to back up that claim." According to Golub, Johnson, Dunlap, and Sifaneck (2004), drug surveillance programs have observed that marijuana use increased and the use of crack, cocaine, and heroin decreased among American adolescents and young adults during the 1990s."(Becca Walls 129) If studies have shown that Marijuana does not necessarily lead to the use of harder drugs that argument frequently used by legislators can no longer be considered viable. If our lawmakers have well considered that a great deal of their arguments have flawed origins in their thesis statements, and those flaws are based in improbable conjecture, they would be morally obliged to withdraw their support of anti-Marijuana legislation. Even when opposing parties are presented with overwhelming evidence contrary to their established beliefs, they may not necessarily take any action to change their vote or publicly change their stance on an issue.

According to Vlahos, Kelley Beaucar the annual cash crop of California Marijuana could be worth in excess of fourteen billion dollars (18). If a state such as Texas could extract thirty percent from fourteen billion over a period of ten years and have that accumulated nest-egg of tax dollars to help with budget shortfalls and the improvement of education facilities the state would certainly have to give more critical thought and attention to the legislative changes. Money is not always a prime motivator, but very influential to constituents as well as lawmakers. If presented with a couple boxcars full of cash, that has been legally acquired and ready to spend, as incentive it would be difficult for lobbyists, legislators not to take a more serious inquiry into what had been considered an definitive negative answer. Hypothetical numbers aside any surplus revenue that could be acquired through Marijuana taxation would be a desirable event considering that revenue does not presently exist. The fact remains that a large percentage of Texas citizens are presently using Marijuana and are not deterred by current laws in that regard, and if tax revenue could be gained from that use it would certainly benefit the state of Texas.

This paper has attempted to explore and discuss the possibility of legalizing Marijuana in the state of Texas. A primary advantage of this type of legislation would be in a reduction of violent crime associated with the sale and importing of Marijuana. The de-criminalization of a controlled substance, historically as in the repeal of prohibition, has lessened the illegal activity formerly associated with that activity. The death toll in border areas where illicit drug trafficking occurs would be reduced.

The medicinal advantages of Marijuana for cancer and aids patients would be an improvement in the quality of life for nausea and lack of appetite sufferers. The medicinal qualities of botanical Marijuana have been documented in reference to their respective levels of (THC).

The de-criminalization of Marijuana would decrease the value of the plant from the perspective of consumer prices. If the Marijuana consumers are paying far less it stands to reason that as the profit margin falls so does the enticement of organized crime factions to continue to be involved in its sale and distribution.

In summation, if the aforementioned reasons for the legalization of medical Marijuana are to be noted as the reduction of violent crime associated with illicit drug sales, the benefit of Marijuana for medical applications, and the de-criminalization and ensuing freeing up law enforcement to move on to other more urgent tasks. It would be logical to assume that the legalization of medical Marijuana would be beneficial to the state of

Texas. One could assume that if something is beneficial and logical that legislators would hurriedly put into effect any law that could reduce crime, help suffering individuals, and quite possibly help law enforcement. Overall this type of legislation would be a great benefit to the citizens of Texas and would hopefully be acted upon sometime in the near future.

Work Cited

Becca Walls, et al. "North Americans' Attitudes Toward Illegal Drugs." Journal Of Human Behavior In The Social Environment 19.2 (2009): 125-141. SocINDEX with Full Text. Web. 23 Oct. 2012.

Bostwick, J. Michael. "Blurred Boundaries: The Therapeutics And Politics Of Medical Marijuana." Mayo Clinic Proceedings 87.2 (2012): 172-186. Academic Search Complete. Web. 23 Oct. 2012.

Cockburn, Alexander. "Obama And Marijuana: A Great Betrayal?." Nation 294.25 (2012): 10. Academic Search Complete. Web. 22 Oct. 2012.

Conant, Eve, and Katie Maloney. "Pot And The Gop." *Newsweek* 156.18 (2010): 30-

35. *Academic Search Complete*. Web. 22 Oct. 2012.

del Bosque, Melissa. "Hyping The New Media Buzzword: 'Spillover' On The Border." NACLA Report On The Americas 42.4 (2009): 46. MasterFILE Premier. Web. 24 Oct. 2012.

Joffe, Alain, and W. Samuel Yancy. "Legalization Of Marijuana: Potential Impact On Youth." Pediatrics 113.6 (2004): e632-e638. Academic Search Complete. Web. 23 Oct. 2012.

Martin Finkel, et al. "Decriminalization Of Cannabis - Potential Risks For Children?." Acta Paediatrica 100.4 (2011): 618-619. Academic Search Complete. Web. 23 Oct. 2012.

New Analysis Of Marijuana Incarceration Data: "Who's Really In Prison For Marijuana" De-Bunks Common

Myths Advanced By Drug Legalization Advocates. Rockville, Maryland, US: White House, Executive Office of the President, Office of National Drug Control Policy (ONDCP), 2005. PsycEXTRA. Web. 23 Oct. 2012.

Feral Hogs Surf Asphalt

The celebrated running of the Hogs on the nation's fastest freeway, on the grassy slopes alongside IH one thirty just outside Austin Texas, lives a population of feral hogs some of which are descended from Russian boars and other boutique swine. These collective swine are lined up to surf the mechanized wave of autobahn vehicles, like Malibu locals waiting for their perfect set of waves. The IH one thirty recently proclaimed the nation's fastest freeway with a speed limit of eighty-five. Bear in mind most drivers take a poetic license with speed limits to presume eight to twelve miles an hour over the posted speed limit as the accepted margin. To set the scene we have three and a half ton vehicles traveling ninety five or more miles an hour and two to four hundred pound hogs running out

into traffic with imminent collisions about to occur. According to the nearest sheriff's department, drivers should not swerve to avoid contact with the hogs, but go ahead and let the collision happen and hope for the best. The sheriff's claim that too many drivers swerve to avoid the hogs and end up in a rollover accident with sometimes fatal results. One would not need a physics lesson to know that a high-speed collision with a large animal and a crumple sensitive sports car is a catastrophic event. If a nine-pound goose can bring down an F-14 then a two hundred pound hog will surely end the journey of a beamer.

The question comes to mind, why are these pigs out here don't they have a farm to go home to, aren't there spiders for them to converse with, is asphalt cold fusion bacon really their future. The reality is these pigs

are lost souls. Their plight of homelessness and being hunted by men in helicopters, when those helicopters aren't too busy ferrying wealthy tourists to Grand Prix races, is one of nomadic wanderings along what is the closest thing to an Autobahn that exists in the U.S... These swine are displaced for various reasons; some wealthy industrialist wants to create a wild game ranch for weekend fun and then imports some Russian Blue boars and other exotics and then his hedge fund evaporates and the exotic animals are left to fend for themselves, others are crossbreeds from farms and ranches that need fences mended and others that are simply wild to begin with.

According to Wildlife Biologist Rick Taylor "There are currently an estimated one million feral hogs in Texas." These hogs are considered a nuisance wildlife

population and are not protected by hunting restrictions by seasonality. They are a danger to small or young livestock such as infant goats or lambs. Their main destruction factor is to agricultural environments by rooting and spoilage of crops by random foraging. Feral hogs can multiply quickly with litters from three to twelve pups and a gestation period of three months from females able to bear at six months of age. (Taylor 5) Although there has been a perennial bounty on these animals little has been done to reduce their current population, due to their natural speed of reproduction.

To examine the supposed thought process of a feral hog, do they see headlights as an enticement to run into what might be a sunrise or an intruder of sorts into the realm of their domain? It might be that there is little or no rational thought to their behavior, and that their

running out into traffic is actually innate behavior to an unknown light source. Mal intent is certainly not in the capabilities of swine; although they are a displaced and hunted population their limited thought process excludes them from deviant behavior.

There was rumor some months ago of a bacon shortage. There might be a probable solution to two different dilemmas. The quality and taste of the flesh of these animals as long as it is carefully prepared is considered by many to be a delicacy. The probability of reducing the population of feral hogs utilizing current methods is unrealistic; however the possibility of examining and innovating methods to market and produce feral hog products is realistic. Instead of hunting and disposing of the feral pigs, with a little fencing and a bit of surplus grain the population could be nurtured and

then harvested to supplant any shortage of pork bellies.

With revenues derived from the sale of Interstate wild bacon a budget could be created to launch a wildlife conservatory habitat where feral populations of the future could be protected.

Feral Hogs Surf Asphalt

The celebrated running of the Hogs on the nation's fastest freeway, on the grassy slopes alongside IH one thirty just outside Austin Texas, lives a population of feral hogs some of which are descended from Russian boars and other boutique swine. These collective swine are lined up to surf the mechanized wave of autobahn vehicles, like Malibu locals waiting for their perfect set of waves. The IH one thirty recently proclaimed the nation's fastest freeway with a speed limit of eighty-five. Bear in mind most drivers take a poetic license with speed limits to presume eight to twelve miles an hour over the posted speed limit as the accepted margin. To set the scene we have three and a half ton vehicles traveling ninety five or more miles an hour and two to four hundred pound hogs running out

into traffic with imminent collisions about to occur. According to the nearest sheriff's department, drivers should not swerve to avoid contact with the hogs, but go ahead and let the collision happen and hope for the best. The sheriff's claim that too many drivers swerve to avoid the hogs and end up in a rollover accident with sometimes fatal results. One would not need a physics lesson to know that a high-speed collision with a large animal and a crumple sensitive sports car is a catastrophic event. If a nine-pound goose can bring down an F-14 then a two hundred pound hog will surely end the journey of a beamer.

The question comes to mind, why are these pigs out here don't they have a farm to go home to, aren't there spiders for them to converse with, is asphalt cold fusion bacon really their future. The reality is these pigs

are lost souls. Their plight of homelessness and being hunted by men in helicopters, when those helicopters aren't too busy ferrying wealthy tourists to Grand Prix races, is one of nomadic wanderings along what is the closest thing to an Autobahn that exists in the U.S... These swine are displaced for various reasons; some wealthy industrialist wants to create a wild game ranch for weekend fun and then imports some Russian Blue boars and other exotics and then his hedge fund evaporates and the exotic animals are left to fend for themselves, others are crossbreeds from farms and ranches that need fences mended and others that are simply wild to begin with.

According to Wildlife Biologist Rick Taylor "There are currently an estimated one million feral hogs in Texas." These hogs are considered a nuisance wildlife

population and are not protected by hunting restrictions by seasonality. They are a danger to small or young livestock such as infant goats or lambs. Their main destruction factor is to agricultural environments by rooting and spoilage of crops by random foraging. Feral hogs can multiply quickly with litters from three to twelve pups and a gestation period of three months from females able to bear at six months of age. (Taylor 5) Although there has been a perennial bounty on these animals little has been done to reduce their current population, due to their natural speed of reproduction.

To examine the supposed thought process of a feral hog, do they see headlights as an enticement to run into what might be a sunrise or an intruder of sorts into the realm of their domain? It might be that there is little or no rational thought to their behavior, and that their

running out into traffic is actually innate behavior to an unknown light source. Mal intent is certainly not in the capabilities of swine; although they are a displaced and hunted population their limited thought process excludes them from deviant behavior.

There was rumor some months ago of a bacon shortage. There might be a probable solution to two different dilemmas. The quality and taste of the flesh of these animals as long as it is carefully prepared is considered by many to be a delicacy. The probability of reducing the population of feral hogs utilizing current methods is unrealistic; however the possibility of examining and innovating methods to market and produce feral hog products is realistic. Instead of hunting and disposing of the feral pigs, with a little fencing and a bit of surplus grain the population could be nurtured and

then harvested to supplant any shortage of pork bellies. With revenues derived from the sale of Interstate wild bacon a budget could be created to launch a wildlife conservatory habitat where feral populations of the future could be protected.

Music Downloading and Effects on the Music Industry

This paper will explore the effect of music downloading on the music industry. To define music downloading briefly as the illegal downloading of recorded digitized music from sources that does not represent or contribute monetarily to the artists from which the music originated. Although there are legitimate websites that sell digitized recordings, they do not represent illegal activity. This work will concentrate on examining entities such as Napster which was at the forefront of the illegal music downloading movement. Napster presented an argument that their format could bolster music sales by exposing many varieties of music that consumers would not normally hear.

(Farshid Navissi Vic Naiker Stewart Upson 167)

However music industry executives claim Napster's responsibility for loss revenue would far out weigh any advantages gained by varietal exposure of different genres of music. With the development of ITunes by Apple in 2003, the music industry had a source of legitimate sales from which to draw revenue from digitized music. Changes to the music industry would be brought on by the digital advancements of recording and processing. Hereafter the tour budgets and promotional activities would be greatly reduced and the golden age of recording would be a thing of the past. The excessive revenue driven activities and subsequent profit margins would be curtailed by the emergence of Internet oriented musical products.

Napster's inception was before any Digital Rights Management (DRM) was enabled. The Internet was wide open and there were no precedents for the governing and policing of digitized music and related items. An entity such as Napster could not be held legally accountable for taking advantage of an opportunity to make a profit where the law had no restriction, although a moral quandary should have them consider the rights of the artists that were not being compensated for their work. There came a flood of Internet consumers that was tailor made for Napster and other internet music sharing providers. These modern internet consumers had little regard for the profit margins of large record companies. The modern young digital music enthusiasts took full advantage of the wide open internet, and built huge libraries of sounds and musical works valued beyond measure to themselves, but highly valuable in lost revenue to the record companies. These types of downloads have changed the music industry tremendously. Daryl J. Woolley from the University of Idaho indicates some astonishing figures regarding downloading:" The total cost of pirating music is estimated at $12.5 billion annually, of which $5 billion is a direct cost to the recording industry."(31) W. Jonathon Cardi relates in a 2007 article from the *Iowa Law Review* "The public proved so hungry for online music that over sixty million Americans turned to a life of crime by way of copyright infringement in order to get their digital fix."(836) the loss of revenues to the music industry has had a vast trickle-down effect. Even roadies and guitar technicians had a 60% reduction in wages when budgets started to dwindle according to George Benson's guitar technichan John Mooy on a recent interview on youtube via the

SeymourDuncanChannel. Mooy also stated that crew members would have to assume more work behaviors than previously expected. In essence the guitar technicians would have to double and sometimes triple their respective workloads by taking on the responsibilities of individuals who had been eliminated by budget constraints. The large budgets were gone and the types of tours and promotions that had been prevalent would be severely altered. Music corporations would have to restructure their marketing, promotions and Artist relations. The wine and dine era has come and gone with smaller overall gross revenue to work with the record labels will have to rethink their complete infrastructure.

    The value of a song by the public perception has become a topic for discussion.

Even if a single song on ITunes costs 99cents it has perceived value below that price. Sandulli and Martin-Barrero relate "that the current price for digital music, on average 99 cents whether dollar or euro, is considered too high by P2P users."(4) If the consumer is unwilling or unmotivated to purchase music at a perceived value that is less than its acceptable market value. Then consumers will be further inclined to download their music rather than purchase it. If market strategies remain where they are the profits will continue to decline and profits will severely decline. The ensuing changes and development of the music industry will be driven by their ability to adjust as the technology dictates.

    Digital Rights Management (DRM) has become a necessary guidance factor in the new music industry. Copyright infringement and digital music ownership have become intertwined with the other problematic facets of profitability in the new music industry. "The economic status of music changes once it can be separated from the tangible object."(Birgitte Andersen · Marion Frenz 716) Changes for the music industry have come from dealing with what was once a physical product to an intangible entity that has value but no physical presence. Although the digitized music product has what could be considered a onetime production cost the relative cost of recording is the same. The post production costs that include manufacturing of disks, tapes, and vinyl records are virtually eliminated. Therefore the profit margin should increase without the post production costs, however with the reduction of overall sales this has not been the case.

A somewhat unsuccessful method of preventing downloading was file pollution. "In order to fight P2P piracy, the recording industry decided to deposit into file sharing networks large volumes of polluted music files."(Sandulli-Martin-Barrero5) These polluted files could include white noise, random distortion, and sound level fluctuations. Sound quality could be differentiated from standard versions by overly compressing or limiting the song selections to create undesirable listening experience. "From a theoretical point of view, pollution reduces significantly the quality of reproduction of the songs, limiting the degree of substitution between the legal song and the illegal one" (Sandulli-Martin-Barrero5) In an industry that is highly dependent on satisfaction of their consumers, the pollution of musical files could be considered a highly improbable proposition, if consumers were to mistakenly receive the polluted musical files. The pollution methods were a considerable deterrent and will continue until better technological methods arise.

The criminalization of individuals who download digitized music, most of whom are minors, has not filled our jails or prisons. Unfortunately the public perception of the illegal music downloading is likened to the taking of soap or towels from hotels, in that it is technically stealing but considered by the general populace to be socially acceptable. These types of illegal activities have not been easy to enforce or gain convictions. Chien-Yi Huang of National Taipei University relates in a recent article "Piracy is the greatest threat facing the global music industry today. Because of the widespread domestic use of high-speed broadband Internet over the past decade, consumers can easily reach, copy from, and upload music to the Internet."(1) However the music industry strives to continue to criminalize and label the offenders as pirates and Internet thieves.

A great percentage of music downloaders are college students age 18-24. In studies done concerning this age group it has been noted that this group has a general dissatisfaction with the music industry as a whole. This peer group has a general perception that the record companies have too large a profit margin. Their beliefs and opinions influence their collective behavior towards downloading and digitized music piracy.

> Several studies indicate that many individuals, particularly young college students, are unsatisfied with the current price of music and.

> Indeed, the price of music and its implications for the consumer are relevant to students' decisions to download music for free For example, found that concerns about price were among the strongest predictors of future intentions to illegally download music, even among students who had never done so before. In addition, found a moderate correlation between beliefs that CD's were not worth the high price record companies charged and previous downloading behaviors.
> (Jambon et all 1)

If their collective belief is that the downloading behavior is not really a criminal act, and record companies have a surplus of profits, then the college students behavior is not really hurting anyone. In summation, the Music industry has been severely altered by the influx of digitized music downloading. The overall profits have been reduced and all aspects of the business have been changed. Budgets for touring musicians have been greatly reduced and the methods for how those tours have been scheduled, and conducted have also been changed. The trimming of spending has caused technicians, sound engineers and other behind the scenes individuals to double up on their respective workloads. The physical changes of the industry, such as no longer having a physical product to manufacture, reproduce and package has created what seems like a better profit margin. However it has been shown that the diminished sales due to music downloading have outweighed any financial gains from reduced production costs.

More Artists can be exposed to the public via the Internet. Music aficionados are able to scan vast websites of choices of musical artists from all over the globe. This gives them an exposure not previously possible before the advent of digitized music. Theoretically, the increase in exposure would help increase sales of songs on the internet, but the typical digitized music consumer has been shown to illegally download rather than purchase especially when their original search was conducted over the Web. The record companies continue to market their digitized product in hopes of swaying the balance against Internet downloading.

Record company executives also are trying to educate prime market groups about the criminalization of music downloading and software piracy. The overall effects of digitized music piracy have been a serious financial burden to the music industry. The subsequent reduction of revenue has been a financial burden to artists, executives, songwriters and al related individuals in the music industry. Profits have been greatly weakened and budgets for tours, artist's development, and production in general. The music industry has been crippled by the insurgence of digitized music downloading.

Work Cited

Andersen, Birgitte, and Marion Frenz. "Don'T Blame The P2P File-Sharers: The Impact Of Free Music Downloads On The Purchase Of Music Cds In Canada." *Journal Of Evolutionary Economics* 20.5 (2010): 715-740. *Business Source Complete*.

Bourreau, Marc. "A Comment On Peitz And Waelbroeck." *Cesifo Economic Studies* 51.2/3 (2005): 429-433. *SocINDEX with Full Text*. Web. 23 Sept. 2012.

Cardi, W. Jonathan. "Über-Middleman: Reshaping The Broken Landscape Of Music Copyright." *Iowa*

Law Review 92.3 (2007): 835-890. *Academic Search Complete*. Web. 23 Sept. 2012.

Chiou, Jyh-Shen, Hsiao-I Cheng, and Chien-Yi Huang. "The Effects Of Artist Adoration And Perceived Risk Of Getting Caught On Attitude And Intention To Pirate Music In The United States And Taiwan." *Ethics And Behavior* 21.3 (2011): 182-196. *Philosopher's Index*. Web. 23 Sept. 2012.

Navissi, Farshid, Vic Naiker, and Stewart Upson. "Securities Price Effects Of Napster-Related Events." *Journal Of Accounting, Auditing & Finance* 20.2 (2005): 167-183. *Business Source Complete*. Web. 23 Sept. 2012.

Sandulli, Francesco D., and Samuel Martín-Barbero. "99 Cents Per Song: A Fair Price For Digital Music? The Effects Of Music Industry Strategies To Raise The Willingness To Pay By P2P Users." *Journal Of Website Promotion* 2.3/4 (2006): 3-15. *Communication & Mass Media Complete*. Web. 23 Sept. 2012.

Rocky Mountain High

The spark of freedom has our nation inhaling a legal Rocky Mountain High.

If Colorado and Washington State can get away with defying the federal government by legalizing marijuana for recreational use, it will set an incredible precedent. Colorado recently passed legislation to legalize marijuana in a recreational form for adults over the age of twenty-one, and in doing so symbolically challenges the federal government to make an objection or forever hold their peace. If states are allowed to pass legislation in direct conflict with federal laws, there will be an unbelievable floodgate opened for new and creative legislation. Were Texas to abolish federal income tax within its borders would Washington DC be inclined to look the other way? States should be allowed to self-govern to a certain extent; however the line that is drawn in the sand has certainly has been crossed by Colorado and Washington State by their recent Marijuana legislation.

It remains to be seen if Drug Enforcement Agency agents will parachute from the sky in a massive statewide raid, exclaiming "hands up citizens if you can see us through the smoke and drug-induced haze you now dwell in". The DEA would be within their rights and jurisdiction to attempt such a raid. The problem for the DEA would be, do they have enough manpower, and if their ranks are lacking, perhaps they can recruit from the nation's unemployed. Our country has a lot of individuals without jobs and healthcare. These recent events concerning drug laws could provide a solution for the nation's economy. Newly deputized DEA agents could have decent paying employment as well as the renowned federal employees' healthcare package. As long as they do not partake in newly legalized Marijuana usage they can stay in good standing with their new Federal employers and possibly be eligible for a favorable retirement package.

If other states were to follow suit and create legislation that was to conflict with existing federal laws and statutes, therein lies a possibility for a nationwide domino effect. The balance of power between the states and the federal government would be completely torn asunder. In order for the federal government to enforce any edicts or directives they would have to recruit more and more individuals to be employed in a massive deployment of unprecedented magnitude in order to staunch the national wound of unrest. On a positive note, a vast recruitment would put a great deal of people to work who currently only utilize their prehensile digits for remote control use, and these new hires would be paying taxes and spending their newly surplus incomes on commodities that would hopefully arouse and stimulate our national economy.

If large raids occurred and vast amounts of marijuana were to be seized, the seized material would have to be catalogued and hopefully put to good use. The medicinal quality components could be reserved for patients who require its healing and nausea-relieving effects. The larger branches and trunk-like material could be utilized for the making of ropes, paper and uniforms for our burgeoning DEA population's training manuals, uniforms and macramé inspired-restraining manacles. Hemp paper products could also be used for official documents and anti-drug propaganda pamphlets. Our government has had a history of making good use of seized materials, and in our current economy it would serve us well to be as frugal as possible.

To make the best of a bad situation has been, or used to be the American way. When danger was near we strengthened our borders or took decisive measures. Now in the face of impending civil unrest due to the collision of state and federal legalities, we must quickly seek a logical and value-driven solution to this legal dilemma. Will it be an unprecedented federal mandate that forces States to repeal legislation that clearly violates federal law? If this type of forced repeal were to occur it would forever change the relationship between states and the federal government. This type of resolution should certainly be avoided if at all possible, because the political fallout would be catastrophic to an already economically weakened nation. In a perfect world the Federal government could lend some legal experts to help states examine possible ways to amend or rescind recent legislation that although liberal and logical in spirit, clearly is more problematic in its implementation and clearly illegal by federal law. In conclusion let us not mar our nation's purple mountain's majesty with a drug induced and legalistic haze.

In the Shadow of Mount Shasta

We wandered through the crisp mountain air towards the horse barn in anticipation of a snowbound trek in the shadow of Mount Shasta. It was not just that you could see your breath; there was also a unique flavor to the air. The flavor of pine and juniper was in the air along with a certain freshness that might bring to mind mint or cinnamon, but in the background of the palate, a subliminal sense response to high altitude atmosphere that has body as well as flavor. Great clouds of exhaled air accompany each step in the frigid mountain air, and each step has its own signature squeak as I tread across the crisp powdery snow. The roofs of the barn and ranch house are completely blanketed with snow and the ground is a white fluffy carpet as far as the eye can see. In the distance the tree line of Silver tipped pines completes a landscape that is dominated by Mount Shasta. In my youth I had seen the silhouette on soda cans and although a familiar shape the aluminum imagery fails miserably in comparison to the majesty of the view that one can behold so close to the ethereal entity. The ancient Indians of the area revered the mountain as a source of creation, and modern cultists believe Shasta to be a point of significant harmonic convergence. There is no doubt of the impressive visage of the view and the wispy crown of stratus clouds adds to the Olympian portrait.

Uncle Jake got one of his hands to saddle a horse for me, being able to ride fairly well, but still enough of a greenhorn to not be trusted to equip the horse for a winters ride in the snow. There was only one horse available and Jake's niece who was my host acquiesced the mount to me. For the sake of poor recollection I will refer to the mount as Shadowfax, as he was capable of galloping through the snow without any visible effort or fatigue. After I had mounted the steed I felt as though I was a character in a surreal film or even a figure in a popular cigarette commercial romping in the frozen tundra with great clouds of exhalations from Shadowfax and myself in a stoic demeanor. I was almost dressed for the part having denim jeans and a North Country wool shirt with a down vest, but alas no Stetson or Winchester to complete the ensemble. I trotted and galloped for as long as I was allowed within the confines of the ranch's fences and brought Shadowfax back to the barn feeling as though I had conquered all of Northern California and Middle Earth as well. The ride was over and the elapsed time escapes me, although the memory stayed vivid for decades.

What could possibly complete a morning such as what I have just described one might ask. With a reasonably short drive through the picturesque mountain country and unequaled vistas along the route home we arrive at our destination. The mountain home of our temporary residence, with its roaring fire place that magically heats the whole house with an ingenious system of furrows in the slab foundation, that disperse heat from the fireplace to all rooms within the house. The instant the front door is opened the warmth beckons you inside, and the smells from the ample kitchen heighten my already voracious appetite. My eyes as well as other senses drank in platters of fried eggs that still have wafts of steam rising from them and the scent of bacon, along with other platters of hash browns and country bacon. Toast already slathered with high grade butter piled high enough to not be dwarfed by the other dishes on the table. A pitcher of fresh squeezed orange juice blushed with cranberry and a pot of prequel Seattle coffee complete the menu. People often speak of a New England or country breakfast as their ideal morning meal; these would pale in comparison to the Northern California breakfast that I had that day. I am not sure how much I ate and have very little memory of the conversation that accompanied the meal. Suffice to say that comfort does not just reside in the cushions of a chair, but in the feelings that come from an exquisite meal and the aftermath of an adventurous morning outing that fulfills the spirit and the intrinsic warmth that comes from a mountain hearth.

Snow day

I am watching the ticker on the bottom of the screen for closings of schools and roads, and low and behold there it is the messiahic message, Eanes is closed and so is Bee Caves road thereby creating the much coveted snow day. I jump up and almost spill my morning dark-roast brew, and proceed to do a touchdown dance somewhere between Chuck Berry's duck-walk and MJ's moonwalk, all without any permanent injury. As soon as the kids found out that school was cancelled, their former sleepy demeanor vanished and they became almost uncontrollably enthusiastic. Snow days rarely occur in Austin, Texas, when they do it seems the thing to do is go outside and embrace the ice and snow, especially if you have children. The year of this photograph escapes me, but the feeling of winters chill and families sharing of Nordic delights has endured the test of time. We dared to dwell under the ice-cycles for a photo opportunity and ended up with a great picture. My daughter had reached her peak height, while my son a full head and shoulders shorter than myself, is almost that much taller than me now, some many years later.

I get the kids and myself as bundled- up as possible and prepare to head out into the frozen wasteland that our yard has become. Parkas, hats, and gloves the seldom used items of warmth are miraculously found. I don my chocolate colored cowboy hat. A hat if you wear for a certain period of time in freezing weather, you can joyfully take off quickly, and watch a miniature steam cloud arise from your head. Sadly on this occasion we were not able to capture this phenomenon. It is surprising how warm a beaver hat can be. I don't want to be considered "all hat no cattle" by my contemporaries, but the warmth provided by such headgear is worth any criticism from neighbors from other parts of the country.

    The air has a different aroma when the temperature falls below a certain range. The cedars seem to permeate the air better around the freezing zone. The invigorating scent of winter is a special treat to the senses. When you walk on a slightly frozen lawn there's a delicious crunch that you cannot hear often enough.

On this particular day there wasn't enough snow to make a snowman. We improvised by making an ice sculpture, thereby ruing my L.L. Bean deerskin gloves I had been carting around since my Boston days. We gathered ice-cycles and other random shards of ice and created a structure similar to Superman's controls in his underground lair. The ice that had formed on the patio table created a large circle to make triangular pieces that the kids enjoyed breaking into decorative shapes. The process was every bit as stimulating as building a snowman, but much more artistic. We took a few pictures and came inside to thaw. The post-thaw feeling of throbbing hands and faces can be eased by copious amounts of hot chocolate laced with marshmallows.

Part of the thrill of a snow day is spending quality time with your children, and the iced-in factor lends a sense of adventure to the situation that would not otherwise be present on a regular day-off. There is also a certain joyful feeling that arises from the spontaneity of an unscheduled day of artic leisure.

Children have a special smile for these types of occasions. It is a smile that cannot be duplicated by television or random rodeo clowns. The type of joy Dani and Jean had on this particular day cannot be re-created or planned regardless of parental imagination.

I don't recall seeing a clock that day. I know that at some point it got dark and soon thereafter we had dinner, which tasted especially great due to the winters celebration. Then we drifted off to a winter's nap of epic proportions.

When we awoke the ice sculpture was greatly altered, and that sculpture was the only remaining ice in the yard.

American Human Trafficking

A nationwide epidemic in human trafficking continues unchecked, despite some efforts by legislators to combat the fast spreading problem. Whether the victims are from the U.S. or foreign countries we need to do everything possible to alleviate the issue. The primary reason for trafficking is the sex trade, but there are many instances of domestic or agricultural labor abuses as well. The efforts to stop the victims from entering the country at border stops are not effective. The police can help when they are made aware of situations, but victims are not always ready to report these crimes due to various reasons. Legislation, such as the Trafficking Victims Protection Act of 2000(TVPA) have demonstrated promising ideals; however their implementation has yielded little success. Further versions of TVPA have shown theoretical improvement and created a field of awareness that did not previously exist. The moral dilemma for U.S. citizens to consider is the reason that the underage trafficked sex trade is rampant here, is because as long as the appetite for this trade exists someone will endeavor to provide the product. There must be a responsible effort to re-educate our population regarding the nuances of the problem and the treatment of those afflicted with deviant sexual appetites.

By definition trafficking is described by Allison Cross from the McGeorge Law Review as "the recruitment, harboring, transportation, provision, or obtaining of a person for labor or services, through the use of force, fraud, or coercion for the purpose of subjection to involuntary servitude, peonage, debt bondage, or slavery."(400) The steps taken to refine and describe the verbiage associated with human trafficking has made the job easier for legislators to begin the task of creating viable laws to combat the rising epidemic. Awareness is essential to creating a successful arena to undertake an active approach to eradicate the human trafficking problem.

The ability of police personnel to recognize victims is essential to prevent dual victimization. Dual victimization exists when human trafficking victims are arrested and prosecuted as prostitutes when their abusers have forced or coerced them to commit illegal sexual acts thereby creating a duality. If the victims are treated as such rather than being treated as criminals and able to be recognized as potential witnesses against their abusers they may have a chance at reentry into normal society. When victims are prosecuted and then released into their former situation the cycle of abuse continues. The problem exists that a great deal of these victims refuses to testify against their abusers. This sometimes occurs because the victim is emotionally involved with their abuser and even in some cases married or related and or adopted, making them unable to differentiate between the assumed loyalty and their own basic rights as free individuals. It has also been observed that many individuals are coerced by threats to family that is not present, but controlled in former residences that their abusers have access to and some hold over. The reality of the extent of the control that some of these abusers have over their victims is shocking to believe, and in some instances unbreakable. The battle would be easier if the police always had the complete cooperation of victims in their attempts to obtain convictions.

The interpretation of prosecution laws are also a factor in the war against human trafficking. If the police are arresting a much greater number of alleged prostitutes and thereby giving an illusion that law enforcement is soft on prostitution consumers. It stands to reason that the consumers are less likely to restrict their deviant sexual behaviors if the penalties are not enforced with the same fortitude as the prosecution of prostitutes regardless of age or trafficking status. Tessa Dysart provides FBI data as follows; "According to the FBI's 2010 Uniform Crime Reports, for jurisdictions that provided information on the sex of those arrested for prostitution and commercialized vice, 68.7 percent of those arrested were females, making it likely that the prostituted person was arrested more often than the buyer."(637) There is a problem inhibiting the successful battle with human traffickers, because there is a conflict of duties where officers have too many tasks that concern possible detainees and prostitutes. From Professor of the Harvard Law Review; "the same persons charged with protecting [victims] are also charged with deporting undocumented persons, arresting prostitutes, and detaining and charging those working without authorization."(*1013*) Subsequent versions of TVPA in first reauthorization in 2003 and then again in 2005 and an additional version backed by President Bush in 2006 which directly addressed domestic minor sex trafficking. For all the criticism George Busch received during his presidency he strongly advocated this bill and demonstrated empathy for the victims it was to protect. The William Wilberforce TVPA of 2008 further strengthened the act by adding provisions for the training of relevant officers to recognize victims of human trafficking and prevent wrongful prosecution and the creation of juvenile residential treatment facilities for the rehabilitation and re-indoctrination into society of victims. Further provisions of TVPA 2008 were the creation of laws with stiffer penalties for offenders who traffic in underage children and the provisions for forfeitures of asset gained in the related criminal activity. Provisions were also created to provide civil remedies and restitution for victims and the designation of sex offender for those who traffic children.

 Conflicting laws between federal and state governments present a unique set of circumstances regarding the prosecution of minors in sex crimes. The federal law states that a minor cannot be charged with prostitution because under federal law a minor prostitute is designated as a sex trafficking victim. However, in many states minor sex trafficking victims have been charged with prostitution and convicted. "In 2010, according to the FBI's Uniform Crime Reports, 804 minors were arrested for prostitution and commercialized vice, including 91 persons under the age of fifteen. Of this number, 656 were females, including 69 girls under the age of fifteen."(632 Dyssart) The Columbia Human Rights Law Review statistics provide a good example of state and federal inconsistencies regarding minor sex trafficking victims (MSTV) and an inability to identify minor sex trafficking victims at the state level. The success at the state level relies on better training of police, prosecutors, social service providers and judges in their treatment of MSTV. Additionally the inconsistency of state minor sex trafficking laws can lead to a migratory procession of traffickers to states with more lenient laws. "According to a NCMEC estimate, 10,000 prostitutes were brought to the 2010 Super Bowl in Miami. Indiana, fearful of a similar situation when it hosted the 2012 Super Bowl, passed a more stringent state trafficking law."(633 Dyssart) Although the problem of state versus federal governments regarding MSTV can become transitory, the real moral issue remains that there is an overzealous appetite for the minor sex trade and the vacationers or sports enthusiasts that are away from home and have an insatiable desire for something that defies all religious and moral codes and ethical behaviors. Yet the real criminals in this issue continue to perpetuate the problem and until they have been re-educated or rehabilitated or received psychiatric treatment to prevent further deviant behavior the MSTV problem will be ongoing.

The child sex trade is big business. According to Dyle of McGeorge Law review; "The Commercial sexual exploitation of children is big business. Sadly, today there is no better return on money than selling a child for sex. The International Labour Office estimates that human trafficking generates at least $32 billion annually" this fact displays the alarming trend of legal leniency towards consumers and perpetuates the cycle of MSTV's. Legal penalties are being raised and conviction rates are still very low. Legislation is taking care of business in regards to tougher stance on MSTV, but enforcement and prosecution are still lagging behind. Identification of victims is the key element in successful processing of MSTVs. Once they are in what should be called protective custody, they must be allowed to sense an element of trust from enforcement officials. The beginning of mutual trust and comprehension will hopefully enable officials to gather intelligence and strategies to prohibit a return to abusive environments and the possibility of gathering testimonial evidence which would increase the conviction rate. One of the biggest drawbacks to increasing conviction rates is the inability to secure successful testimonial evidence from MSTVs. This inability could be because MSTVs have an inordinate amount of misplaced loyalties to their abusers. Sometimes the loyalties are due to relationships based on co-dependence or illusionary romance brought on by perpetrators intentional psychological conditioning and even drug dependency and subsequent staged withdrawal.

As in any high profit business the strategies are not accidental and the recruitment processes are dictated by consumer demand. The demand has steadily increased over the last decade the methods of the perpetrators have become more sophisticated and the people at the top of the food chain have continued to further insulate themselves from the lower levels thereby securing there longevity in their criminal endeavors.

The proprietors of the sex trade are motivated by greed and the highest dollar transactions frequently are associated with underage subjects. While this fact does not stem from any logical human condition or psychological abnormality it makes it hard to define and identify the consumers of the underage sex trade. They are not all obvious sexual deviants that are reminiscent of novel characters we are all so familiar with. A great deal of these sexual deviants are our neighbors and sometimes even family or friends. We fail to recognize the hidden behaviors and sometimes intermittent activities of these people because they are our friends, neighbors and family, and are not necessarily subject to a great deal of scrutiny towards deviant sexual behavior. These types of sexual desires are not unique to metropolitan environments and could be equally prevalent in urban and rural areas as well. The rehabilitation of these deviants is essential to the successful reduction of the MSTV dilemma. The identification and subsequent processing, conviction and rehabilitation of these criminals can only be achieved by careful and diligent police and other law enforcement individuals If possible when MSTVs are apprehended a DNA trail can be created to identify any person or persons that have relations with the victim. In order to establish this type of trail the DNA database would have to include sex offenders and those possible offenders that had previously plea bargained their conviction to lesser charges. In the event that former sex offenders are paroled and rehabilitated their DNA profile will always be in a sex crimes database that could be continually updated to include viable suspects as well. As science progresses the eventuality of an international database of DNA signatures secured at birth will create an unmistakable trail to the violators of underage children and young adults. These prospective methods will invariably cause uproar in human rights violations and will also create a moral dilemma in regards to violation of someone's personal privacy against the protection of MSTVs and other related crime victims.

The eventuality of further legislation to follow the progression of TVPA bills and the development of State's whom have also created bills to protect MSTVs in their respective Sates the Human Trafficking problem will hopefully be reduced and kept somewhat in check. Although human trafficking is a nationwide problem and addressing the issue by pointed legislation is admirable, the root of the problem is the deviant sexual appetite of parts of our population, and until this aspect has been addressed the legislation will only accomplish keeping politician's legislative records looking good for their constituents. The deterrents created by later versions of TVPA are commendable in their proactive clauses that can label offenders as sex offenders and the asset confiscation aspect would hopefully intimidate the intended criminal element. However, unfortunately the targeted criminal element is rarely in the proverbial sights of our law enforcement officials. The upper echelon of the sex trade crime lords have thoroughly insulated themselves from the business end of the criminal activity, and have also erased the monetary trail that would tie them to any illegal activity. The federal law definition of child prostitution as trafficking is a commendable attribute to recent legislation and if the State governments would adhere to this definition the frequency of MSTVs being prosecuted for crimes that the Federal government has stipulated as victimization rather than prostitution, there would be a chance for more rehabilitation and placements in social service facilities. The accurate and decisive identification of MSTVs and sexual deviants in their respective rolls will have a more positive effect on the MSTV problem by eliminating unnecessary prosecutions and facilitating the successful convictions and subsequent rehabilitations of sexual deviant offenders.

    Americans need to take a close examination of existing deviant behaviors in our society and their long term effects on the youth of our country. If the influential and governing entities of America turn a blind eye to these types of problems and continue to ignore the issues that chip away at the foundation of our society. It is the moral responsibility of every American to concern themselves with the protection and safety of our younger population. This responsibility includes a dedicated sense of diligent awareness towards moral issues concerning American youth and their educational and moral development without and deviance or criminal encumbrances related to MSTV and related issues.

Santa Cruz

It was a foggy morning in Santa Cruz, but of course when was it not foggy in a northern California beach town in the morning. There was a fog in the air and a fog in our heads. The previous night's revel had lasted late into the night and you could hear the foghorns from the bay. Evidently the seamen were early risers and blew their horns without any respect for our foggy and swollen heads. The smell of the sea mixed with the scent of the local fauna was familiar from many previous visits to Santa Cruz. Manzanita and Pine along with a mix of other trees made for an interesting scent unique to Santa Cruz.

We were staying at my friend's parent's beach house and it was spring break. Nine or more high school students crammed into the house bunkhouse style. It was one of many beach houses that were of various associations. Some were summer houses of the parents of people we knew, and others such as my aunts, were family places that did not usually welcome or tolerate spring breakers.

    My fellow revelers were still sleeping and it was a good time for a walk on the beach. Most of the aforementioned houses were actually on the beach, except for the one where we stayed on that particular trip. So it was more than a few strides to get to the beach. Once on the beach I headed toward the boardwalk, walking on the waterline where the sand is a little firm and the scent of the sea is mixed with the fragrance of seaweed that has accumulated during the night. The morning is a great time at the beach. The crowds are not around and the usual noise factor was gone. The solitude of a walk on the beach at sunrise was uplifting in a strange sort of way. The problems that are usually pondered seem a little less daunting when you are strolling on the sand. The rhythm of the waves was therapeutic. Decisions that were being debated within one's mind, such as, what to do about college were less threatening.

The view of the mountain range that surrounds the area became readily apparent when the fog started to lift. The coastal range frames the beach with panoramic belt of evergreen foliage. The Santa Cruz Mountains stretch from just south of San Francisco to the north and to the Pajaro River to the south. The area is incredibly fertile and some of the finest wine grapes were grown there. What had begun as a mission town had blossomed into a popular beach resort that included California's oldest boardwalk.

It was time to turn around and head back to the beach house. Someone would have been awake to go out to breakfast. Although the beach house was fully equipped I do not remember anyone ever cooking anything there. The family that owned the house was once the largest beef producing family in the western United States, and it seemed that a barbecue grill would have been almost required, but there was none. Once back at the house I found a couple awakened compatriots to accompany me to Luther's. Luther's was one of those unique breakfast places that every small town should have. It was a very small diner style restaurant that puts out reasonable priced food with simple dignity for a nominal charge. There were no table tents advertising products that could be construed as promotional. There was no canned music, just a simple diner with excellent food that usually arrived quickly. Eggs over-easy and hash-browns and toast, along with some crude oil coffee and the day was ready to begin. The resumption of the revelry would have begun sometime after breakfast.

My associates for spring break were all from the local private Catholic school in our home town. We had been working together at a construction site, which oddly enough was owned by one of their classmate's father. One the day when we collectively asked off for the block of time for spring break we were collectively fired. So leaving our future in the construction business behind us, we began our sojourn to the coast from the flatlands of the San Joaquin valley. We packed the necessities that did not include food and commenced the epic journey. The drive from the center of the San Joaquin valley to Santa Cruz takes a little over three hours or the ninth loop of a Van Morrison eight-track cassette. I know this to be true because on another beach mission we listened to Moondance the entire trip, and had it been any other music album of lesser quality I might not have survived. Finally we arrived at our destination and unpacked our gear and surprisingly enough, we did not open windows and fluff pillows as most people do when opening a rarely occupied dwelling. Instead we stowed away our beverages in the fridge and headed almost immediately for the beach. It was a ten minute walk to the beach and another ten to the boardwalk.

Even though we were a brotherhood of sorts we sought companionship of the sisterhood variety. Some of which that we met were from our town, but a different high school. It seemed strange that we would meet a group that was only five miles from where we lived, but they were nice girls and the three sisters from their group were very unique. The sisters were brunettes with sky blue eyes and dimples that would make you laugh. They seemed to collectively possess a sense of self that defied embarrassment. A definite grasp of living in the moment that was utterly charming, they seemed to like spending time with us and we kept in touch for a while after we returned home.

There is a myth about California beaches. Part of the myth is that people can swim and surf comfortably in the ocean. This a bit of propaganda more than likely created by the film industry at the request of the tourist bureau. The water is very cold and the further out you go the colder it is. I remember swimming in Santa Cruz in the summer and having my feet ache because of the cold.

When you view footage of people surfing in California without a wetsuit it probably was filmed elsewhere or the actors were getting extra pay for their suffering. Although the water is very cold it smells of Abalone and Pine. It also tastes of minerals other than salt, whether this because of unreported oil or chemical spills is anyone's guess.

The texture of the sand is different from other beaches. The sand seemed a touch finer than other beaches. There were no Dunes, but the sand extended quite a bit up the width of the shore. Just a few feet from the water line it was difficult to run, and there were just enough crustacean shells intermingled with the sand to keep your feet wary. The lifeguard towers were spread every hundred yards or so, and they were approximately eight feet high. The height is etched in my memory because I jumped off the top of one and thought I had ruined my knee. As it turned out it was only a light sprain and an easy payment for a reckless act of youth.

The Pier at Santa Cruz is old and creaky. It also possesses a great view of the area. There are shops and restaurants, bait shops, and interesting people to watch. The Pier also smells of dead fish, French fries and oily wood. It also smelled as though someone failed to make it to the restroom in time. It may have been that people were frustrate by the lack of personal facilities and were careless with their waste water. The Pier was a great place for fishing and crabbing. We mostly were crabbers. It was probably because all we needed was some string and bait, where fishing required more equipment than we could muster. On one occasion when we were crabbing we saw an errant pelican crash into a post. This seemed very strange because in general pelicans seem to be very good flyers and quite dexterous in their fishing and stunt-like aerial abilities. So we were almost speechless when the pelican hit the post. The bird did not pierce the post with its bill as one might expect, but slammed the telephone-like post, fell to the ground and flopped around for a minute and then walked off in a zigzag fashion. We looked at each other with the unspoken question of whether or not the event we witnessed had really happened. We left the Pier that day with a different opinion of Pelicans and of course no crabs.

The celebratory bonfire was a matter of great excitement. There was no careful planning or safety procedures. We simply gathered enough dry driftwood to build a fire and dug a makeshift pit in which to house the fire somewhat responsibly. We were aware that too big a fire would attract undesirable attention from the local police, with whom we sought as little contact as possible. There was always a little too much damp wood in the fire and this made for a smoky side to the fire. So I tried to keep ahead of the smoke, but it seemed to follow me around the fire almost as though the smoke was stalking me. The conversation around the fire seemed to follow no particular course or direction, and the participants would speak louder and louder without listening to each other. The fire would always include songs from "American Graffiti" with a loose waiver for the semblance of pitch and meter. Enthusiasm would trump talent at the bonfire and there was an illusion that volume would enhance quality.

    The Santa Cruz Boardwalk was an iconic amusement area. It had a wood framed rollercoaster and actual wood framed pier to accompany it. An overhead tram that ran the length of the Boardwalk was a great way to relax and get a great view of the area. The mixture of aromas was varied between the smell of the salt air with the scent of cotton candy, popcorn, diesel, and the sweet smell of countless sodas spilled by the patrons of the Boardwalk. The arcades with the destined to lose games, along with the more infamous rides such as the bumper cars and the Roundup were more popular with our group. The Roundup was a circular ride with strap-in sections along the interior of the circle. When the ride began it would spin at a fast rate and then slowly tilt till it reached ninety degrees of its axis. As the axis was reached the wind coming in off the ocean would rock the structure slightly terrorizing the riders by the unexpected aspect of the ride. It felt as though the whirling circle was being ripped from its mountings by the wind and I remember screaming to the attendant to stop the Roundup. Countless attendees had probably screamed to stop this ride or another and my plea was unanswered.

Trips to Santa Cruz were always special. Unfortunately, how special they were was not as readily apparent at the time. In the mindset of youth one did not always take the time to cherish the moment, or drink in the smells of trees, salt air or take a mental picture of the surroundings for later examination. We lived for the moment, and did at times appreciate where we were despite the fast living appetites and behaviors of our existence. Santa Cruz was the paradise we chose.

Santa Cruz Harmonic Convergence

There is a cell of very creative luthiers in Santa Cruz California, a veritable nest of tonal geniuses all working in the approximately the same geographical location in the production of fine acoustic and electric guitars, ukuleles, and similar instruments. The instruments they produce are unique in their appearance as well as their tonal signature. If a certain location can produce the inspiration for superior design and construction of fine guitars and their similar counterparts, then Santa Cruz has achieved that status. The exchange of ideas and sometimes exclusively essential equipment and ensuing results is similar to the Socratic era of Greek city States in its creative and inspirational environment.

Richard Hoover of Santa Cruz Guitar Company (SCGC) is one of the earliest builders of guitars in the Santa Cruz area. His acclaimed instruments have graced stages and studios all over the world. SCGC, created in 1976, has produced excellent guitars and also, through its apprentice program, acclaimed luthiers. Scott Walker, of Scott Walker Electric Guitars, started as an apprentice at SCGC after graduating from Roberto Venn Scholl of Luthiery in Phoenix, Arizona. Another renowned luthier in the area is Rick Turner of Renaissance Guitar and former founding partner in Alembic Guitars that was made famous by Jerry Garcia, Steven Stills and other artists. Turner is also well known for his innovations and developments of signal processing within guitars and his creation of pickups that produce a more realistic and cleaner sound for acoustic and electric guitars.

Turner's Model-one which Lindsay Buckingham of Fleetwood Mac made iconic by his endorsement and continued usage on stage during touring. Model-one shares the tonal qualities of a stellar acoustic with the searing tones of a vintage electric without any of the feedback concern associated with stage acoustics in large concert and stadium venues. The switching of guitars during verses and choruses of songs was eliminated for Buckingham by the creation of the Model-one, because of the guitars ability to change from acoustic to electric tone by controls at a finger's touch on the guitar itself, thereby eliminating the necessity and distraction of guitar technicians racing on and off stage during the course of a song. The tonal clarity and ease of switching coupled with the unique style of Buckingham's playing made the Model-one a creative success. Turner's creation of the Renaissance guitar stage acoustic with zero feedback and concert quality sound was another example of his intuitive ability to re-engineer the signal processing and manufacturing process to build an affordable stage acoustic that sounded and played like one's favorite dreadnought without the usual concerns of large venue amplification. Turner's creation of the Compass Rose acoustic guitar with a flying buttress system of bracing, graphite rods, and innovative neck attachment design that aids in the deployment of tonally selected woods that reduce weight and heighten sustain and frequency range.

    Rick moved to Santa Cruz in 1997 partly because he had begun to outgrow his shop in Topanga Canyon and also because he wanted to raise his child in a different atmosphere. The child's godfather, British musician Martin Simpson who was a Santa Cruz resident, suggested that Rick and family relocate to Santa Cruz. Along with the urging of luthier Richard Hoover from SCGC, the Turners left Topanga Canyon for Santa Cruz without regrets. Turner now works out of a 3500 sq. foot facility and produces twenty-five instruments a month. Turner enjoys the interaction with other local luthiers and, as he states, the occasional "careful restoration of unique instruments". In a recent interview Turner states, "I do enjoy working with special woods" and further relates the story of a Giant Sequoia that had fallen on UC Santa Cruz land in 1968 and was in embattled litigation for many years due to it being a forbidden to harvest status, and he stated, "it was 283' high and 27' in diameter and over 2700 years old, the wood was very fine grained and very deep red, and quite resonant." He described the wood as someone else might describe a rare wine or a forgotten Rembrandt, with a quietly stated reverence and enthusiasm. He further related that he had built "several ukuleles and three Model-ones" with a tone of respect for the unique elements and creations. Turner still performs with a band called the"Uke Ellingtons" with a style that the name made obvious. Even after a long, storied career in the creation of fine instruments, Turner still keeps his talented hands in the day-to-day operation and only employs four other craftsmen in the production team.

    Richard Hoover is the creator and owner of SCGC. He has been building guitars and training master luthiers for many years. His expertise in guitar building is almost unparalleled. If he did not reside or work in Santa Cruz there would be no one close to his ability in close proximity. Hoover has sustainability awareness for the products that he uses. He states in a virtual tour of the SCGC facility," the problem with irresponsible harvesting that removes a tree from an ecosystem, it also affects the livelihood of the local inhabitants" Hoover also related," we would not be part of deforestation." Hoover has a dedicated awareness to the path from forest to purveyor to luthier, and primarily utilizes reclaimed wood from reliable sources.

Hoover has an extended knowledge of not only modern luthiery, but also the practices of Italian master violin makers. The ancient violin makers had a vision of extended the value of an instrument by building with an awareness of future generations that would be playing an instrument, and taking precautions in construction that would not only extend the life of the instrument, but also ease the probability of restoration by employing natural glues and construction methods that would facilitate the likely restoration endeavors. Hoover's tonal creation applications include hand tapping every piece of wood to analyze its tonal range and modifying the build to ensure the best tonal application. Hoover has compared the mass production methods of robotic engineering the wood to create guitar kits to" throwing rocks at a piano with your eyes closed… eventually you might hit a chord." Hoover knows what a guitar that SCGC builds will sound like before it is completed. Even though no two guitars will sound alike, he will have a very good idea as to what the tonal range, frequency range, and the type of sustain the guitar will exhibit. SCGC's adherence to responsible harvesting along with its dedication to producing the best instrument possible makes them one of the premier luthiers in the world, not just Santa Cruz.

Scott Walker began his own guitar shop after apprenticing at SCGC. He knew from the beginning that he did not want to build "three hundred dollar guitars." Walker knew he wanted to build ultimate guitars. Guitars with the widest frequency range, the longest sustain and an effortless playability, guitar characteristics that had been ingrained through countless conversations with artists, and also with his own personal experience as a guitar player. As shop foreman at SCGC, Scott oversaw a great deal of custom work, interfaced with top guitar players, and learned what they were seeking in their instruments. With the care and scrutiny of all hand-built parts, Scott currently turns out twenty-five instruments a year. When asked about the interaction between Santa Cruz luthiers, Walker described the results as "cross pollination". These luthiers are artists and, as such, they are not constantly looking over each other's shoulders; however, there is a great deal of sharing of ideas and sometimes equipment. Walker sometimes takes his guitars to Turner's shop to use his specialty sprayer. A great deal of modern luthiers utilizes nitro-cellulose for finishing their guitars. It is an organic compound that is plant-based and possesses a better tonal response than urethane, which is more commonly used in high production guitar making. Walker's use of Turner's sprayer is evident of a desire to facilitate the best and most efficient method of finishing his instruments. There is a lot of handwork in the creation of fine guitars and these luthiers Walker, Turner, and Hoover; fabricate their own jigs and other specialized tools for the work in their respective shops. An inherent enthusiasm for the materials and the designs they employ makes these luthiers unique. They are artists. The creations they fabricate could easily hang in museums or be mounted in hermetically sealed glass cases. Instead, each creation is almost a living being. The wood breathes. With the right handling, the guitar can sing. They are also immortal. In the right environment, a guitar could last an eternity; if treated properly a guitar can survive multiple generations and provide a unique voice for each respective generation. A guitar will slowly alter in sound quality as it ages. The timbre of the guitar's voice will mellow with age, and as it ages the guitar will sustain longer to a certain extent. When builders such as Walker approach a new project they are seeking the utmost for the customer; and conversely, the modern boutique buyer has high expectations for the premium price that is required. Guitars in the five- thousand and up range are a small market share; however, the buyers of these instruments are patient for the build which might take as many as six months to a year, yet they are also very critical in appearance, performance, and tonality of the product they receive. Buyers that put down fifteen hundred dollars to get on the production list, then an additional fifteen hundred to begin the project, and then pay the balance prior to shipping, expect everything to be perfect on arrival.

      Kenny Hill is another Santa Cruz luthier. Hill's specialty is classic guitars. His evolution in guitar building includes a stint in Pachaco, Mexico where he studied with Mexican masters for eight years. Hill has developed a double top method that utilizes wood layers of wood with a layer of Nomex in between; this process enhances the projection ability of the guitar. Hill has also pioneered a venture to build guitars in China that are more affordable than his hand-built signature series, but not the lower quality associated with Chinese mass production. Hill's signature guitars are uniquely patterned after classic guitar builders Hauser, Torres, and

Fleta. These assimilations have been painstakingly created after studying drawings of an 1836 Hauser that was a favorite of Segovia. An excerpt from an article written by Hill explains his thoughts on the double top method he employs.

> I constructed the soundboard using two thin layers of wood separated by a layer of a honeycomb material called Nomex, but then I used a pretty conservative bracing system. What the heck, maybe I could get the best of both worlds. But then we come to the first question. When you go to a restaurant, the first question is, "Do you want ice water?" With classical guitars, the first question is, "Spruce or cedar?" Well, it's both. That's a cool thing with the laminated soundboard: finally I could use both spruce and cedar so I didn't have to

ask that question anymore. But of course now I have to ask "Is the spruce on the outside or the inside?"(Hill)

Hill also related a story about a customer that was not getting the frequency response from his vintage 1937 Hauser.

> Speaking of ears, a guy in Southern California bought one of my '37 Hauser models through a dealer. I started getting e-mails saying "What can I do about the highs? It doesn't have any highs." And I thought "If any guitar has highs, that thing does." He lived eight hours away, but he didn't want to ship it. He said he would make the trip up and bring the guitar to me. Then I didn't hear from him for a while. One day an e-mail popped up. It said, "You might remember me. I was complaining

about my Hauser with the bad highs. I went to the doctor and he pulled a 2" plug of wax out of my ear. Now can you make any suggestions for a change in strings? The thing sounds too bright. (Hill)"

Hill has been published numerous times in various publications and has also taught at University of California at Santa Cruz. He splits his time between the boutique shop in Santa Cruz, the management of the plant in China, and teaching guitar-making classes. Hill's unique perspective is that he builds hand-made classical guitars that take a year to finish as opposed to the partnership in China that turns out guitars in a matter of weeks.

The luthiers of Santa Cruz create unique instruments that are tonally diversified and visually stunning. Richard Hoover best described the custom guitar building process as," complementary materials and a dedicated group." It would not seem to be a coincidence those creative minds and hands gravitate to a unique and idyllic location, such as Santa Cruz, to conduct their business of fine instrument crafting. Their respective instruments produce a harmonic convergence of a different magnitude, and un-paralleled by known regions. Their convergence on the area could be accidental, but the quality of the harmonics their respective instruments produce certainly is not. Their interaction, although not regimented is an enhancement to their creativity. Walker describes the interaction as "cross pollination", and Hoover calls it "symbiosis", but however it is labeled, the interaction is a contributing factor to their respective success.

The author had spent summers, spring breaks, and adult vacations in the Santa Cruz area. The fascination and rapture for the natural beauty of the area has been exceeded by the knowledge of the underlying creative force of the inhabitants. The successes of the Santa Cruz luthiers are the tip of the proverbial iceberg in relation to the mass of local artisans, writers, and academics that reside there. It will hopefully not be long before the writer again visits Santa Cruz.

Stockton beach

The water looked like a maelstrom of micro rainbows and arced splashes,

and yet there were patches of open water, still and shinning like glass.

Visions of celestial hail storms with crimson sashes.

The scent of lilac permeates the salty air.

Oceans transcend into rivers that refract the sky with cloudy patches.

A hum of voices eclipses the silence.

Light penetrates the mirror surface with prismatic rods and crystal lashes.

These visions of buried thought are apparent to those without despair

Lexicon of Prose

11/7/2013
Daniel Haverty

Lexicon of Prose

Daniel Haverty

11-7-2013

ISBN:

978-1-304-66450-1

The Last Horn

*Someone screamed stat. "Give me the cardio-epi or this show is over. Get off those Ski-boots so I can see the toes. We need a full set of cranial scans **yesterday**. How long was the flight off the mountain? Vitals are scary, can we get an EEG asap. If we don't see brainwave activity we'll need some authorization to continue life-support."* Calm and warm it seems like an audience of one for hospital dinner theatre. A luminescent tunnel beckons me onward. I feel as though I could travel through time and space. The tension below doesn't affect me as I don't feel attached to that scene anymore. I drift without moving... *"He's crashing charge the paddles and ready, clear...bang, once again ready, clear, bang"*

Pushing with each ski in a skating maneuver to gain quick acceleration I head down the deserted slope and accelerate rapidly. I crouch into a tuck position with elbows at my sides and knees pressed to my chest, and skis eighteen inches apart, thus creating the most aerodynamic profile for the assault down the mountain. I head into the first long roundhouse turn which can be managed without sacrificing any speed and staying compressed in order to maintain maximum speed heading into the steep sidewinder ahead. The roar of the wind is intense, and the chattering of the skis edges as they hold the suddenly icy slope and a large rooster tail of shredded snow follows me like a shadow as I descend further down the mountain. My thighs are starting to burn as fatigue sets in, and a certain rubbery feel to the legs permeates my thoughts, but I must remove these thoughts from my mind as any deviance from total concentration at this point will spell ruin. As the crest of the next ridge approaches I know the steepest is yet to come, as I have covered these slopes for countless runs in the past. The wind is screaming as I descend further and the slope nears a more vertical profile, and I accelerate even more with heart pounding and legs burning. I do not surrender to the discomfort and forge further down the mountain towards what has been nicknamed the camel bumps. The trick to the camels is to pre-jump the first in the series and take a little distance from the second without too much height, because if you do not address the camels correctly they will devastate you by causing spectacular crashes. I take a little hop over the first camel and jump the second sailing thirty meters in the air, but only a few feet off the ground and land gently tuck position intact.

Two hundred pairs of eyes directed at me with the utmost vehemence and absolute hatred, it would have been more easy to bear if there were a seat at the front of the bus, but these assembled teachers and students had been waiting an hour and a half in a somewhat diesel-choked bus, and had become very angry with the cause of their delay, whose death march to the back of the bus seemed to take an eternity. Not a word was spoken and none were necessary as the eyes of the gathered pierced me with messages of extreme loathing. A light layer of snow was falling which would require chains on a public vehicle adding another forty-five minutes to a return trip that would already be an eternity, because of the cloud of repugnance in the air.

When the Claxon sounds the mountain is closed. The sharp bark of the Claxon horn can pierce the mountain air and be heard for miles and those on the slopes should be aware that the chairs will stop running and the ski patrol will wait a compulsory twenty minutes and sweep down the mountain looking for stragglers. This routine occurred at five pm or dusk depending which happened first. To wait for the patrol to pass and have the trail to one's self was the ultimate goal. To blaze down a pre-chosen path as though it were a downhill course and carry as much speed as possible all the way to the bottom, finishing with a snow spewing final flourishing skidding stop.

More than halfway down the mountain and still accelerating, always looking for the fastest line of descent, I continue the run despite the growing pain in my legs. One or two luge-like turns and I will be heading towards a straight-line finish. I power into the last series of turns holding position and riding high into the bank of the turn, I catch an edge briefly and set the ski back down gently as to make no sudden moves at this speed. I enter the last turn if I can hold form here I can make it without a serious crash, and at speed approaching forty-five miles an hour crashes are to be avoided at all costs.

Badger Pass in Yosemite National Park was a short bus ride from Clovis California and once in a while a destination for Junior High Field trips. This was the case in the winter of seventy-three. A group was assembled at a pre-selected parking lot and a precursory role was taken and the generic Greyhound took off for the Sierra Mountains. With a large group there are typical songs to be sung and adolescent hijinks to be performed, but generally speaking the two and a half hour bus ride was uneventful. The same trip up the mountain could be accomplished in two hours or less depending on who was driving. There was also no ice chest to snack from as was the routine in a family car and other differences would become apparent later that day.

We grabbed our skis and other equipment and rushed off for the lift line. In the mad dash from the diesel choked parking lot to the more pristine lodge and chairlift areas there had been some semblance of rules, procedures and other directions from our illustrious teacher chaperones that were somewhat ignored by the excited teens. One of which to be found out later was an imposed curfew of three-thirty sharp, to meet back at the bus equipment et all. Typically at fifteen years old one does not cherish time spent in the realm of nature's beauty, instead the tribe of Nordic sportsmen would ski as fast as possible and try to accumulate as many runs down the mountain as possible, even skipping lunch if that were imaginable for teenagers. The skill level was diverse amongst this group. Some were skiing fast and falling a lot and could be described as tumbling down the mountain and skiing a little in between tumbling runs, while others could only manage to be upright for a brief few seconds at a time. These skill differences created a separation from classmates and those who could ski fast and error free were soon not among their Nordic compatriots for the duration.

As the apex of the turn approaches I am feeling elated and fatigued at the same time. The pain of exertion in my legs has turned to numbness, and even the cold mountain air is burning my lungs as the run comes to a close. I am trying to hold my line through the turn as the suddenly much icier conditions are becoming treacherous. My skis are bouncing instead of holding the line firmly and my stamina seems to be disintegrating as the conditions worsen. It is becoming almost dark and the bumps are much harder to see in the mountain twilight, this can cause mistakes, and the icy snow is much like concrete as far as forgiveness goes. Time seems to have slowed as I am holding my line through the turn, it feels as though the action is slow motion, but the sound of the wind screeching and my heart thumping like a disco kick drum are in real time. I exit the turn and continue with the bumps, which are now virtually unseen, bouncing me up and down precariously as my skis track towards the finish.

Splashdown

It was like being caught in the bottom of a waterfall with a tumbling of bodies and continual motion that was unpredictable, savage yet controlled. The exertion factor was at a premium. Where the action was taking place the water looked like a maelstrom of micro rainbows and arced splashes, and yet there were patches of open water, still and shinning like glass. From a distance the pool looked as though a pod of dolphins were having a rumble with their rivals. It was sunny for a winter's day and the habitual morning fog had long since departed. When the first whistles were blown the weather was perfect for the action at hand. The first whistle began a dual sprint opposing players start from opposite ends, and the ball is placed in the middle of the pool. If you dig very hard with every stroke and kick like

Neptune is chasing you, the ball can be won and possession achieved. That being accomplished we score rather quickly after a series of quick passes. When competing against an overmatched opponent there is a tendency to play down or subconsciously commit uncharacteristic errors. If you let them think they are in the game, then to some degree they are. This contest between highly ranked and unranked does not proceed as expected and what should have been a scrimmage like atmosphere becomes a desperate struggle of leviathan-like proportions. The score is close enough to still pull out a victory albeit an embarrassing one. Cinch down the defense and create some turnovers and with superior speed and agility this contest will be over. Sometimes in the course of an athletic endeavor the internal dialogue can slow down as oxygen debt is approached, where the seven seconds it takes to cover twenty meters in a pool can seem like minutes or even hours in extreme situations.

This was one of those periods of time that lasts longer than it should and dwelled in memory even longer. Playing very tight defense in the closing moments would yield a turnover and the time was ripe to take off like a trophy fish that will not be caught. Taking a little poetic license with a push off the hip, because an obvious push from the chest will result in an offensive foul we cannot have at this juncture. Number three is out on the break churning water as though there is a tow rope underwater; being caught is not a reality. Too much speed and distance for the possibility of being overtaken, though someone always trails in hopes of the unthinkable, unforeseen happenstance. Athletes at this level do not run out of gas, swimming fifteen to twenty thousand meters a day will insure that.

Time has now slowed almost to a dead stop. The sounds and cheering and yelling have become a whale's baseline with no discernible breaks. Taking a look backwards for the sight of the ball arcing downward ever so slowly, but accurate as though guided by a laser it lands a few feet in front of the chin, but not so far away for a goalie to come out from his cage and intercept it. Breakaways are the stuff that makes practicing for games entertaining; it becomes second nature after thousands of repetitions. As the goalmouth approaches one will juke to one side and more than likely shoot to the other, providing the goalie has not already committed to one side or the other. These scenarios and probabilities have been addressed countless times and drilled out of the realm of reaction rather than deduction. The long hours it seemingly took to swim twenty meters has elapsed and the ball already having arrived it is time to deliver it to its destination and end this troublesome foray. With a quick shift from right hand to left hand, and drill the rock out of this dimension, to propel the ball with the utmost velocity in a predestined visualized target location within the goal. With all the force of a Faulkner phrase the ball hits the crossbar and rebounds harmlessly away, with no chance for a rapid second shot. The clock runs out and Portland State has a moral victory with a tie.

The pool at this end has a sixteen foot depth, and there are observation windows for those curious souls that yearn to know what actually happens underwater. Swimming down to the bottom is a temporary evasion; alas the windows do not open like submarine hatches.

The stench of a grievous error is discernible even at this depth. If one could obtain some diving gear perhaps one could remain in this underwater shelter till the players have left and the crowd dispersed. Or even sneak out to an unfamiliar dining hall and then trek up into the high Sierras till the unthinkable is forgotten. If your psyche is torn asunder, how long will it take to heal? The cranial burn is very intense. The vivid and intensely painful recollection of this recent error is an example of the human ability to punish itself. The wrath of the internal dialogue can be merciless by repeating an event within the mind over and over like an overzealous video tape editor with a penchant for repetition, reliving the capsule in a timeless loop always wishing for another outcome that never transpires. Sometimes a herculean effort of a physical nature will provide temporary relief, such as five sets of forty handstand pushups, which had been a frequent remedy for the author and subject of this recollection. A weekend or even a month or two, it might even take thirty years to forgive oneself for an event that has only the value to which one gives it. Stockton, California and the University of the Pacific are thousands of miles away now, but the memories that were etched in the mind there are never very far away.

Leaf Blower Nation

As a landscaper employs a leaf blower to blow the leaves from an assigned area and never picks them up, to a nation that fixes problems by moving monies or assets to another area is avoiding the root problem. The mess simply moves to another area, as unfortunately our government seems to move assets or bail out conglomerates while we have people losing their homes and children going hungry. While the bailout money is used to fund corporate retreats and incentive bonuses for executives, the plight of middle America is accentuated by this sweep it under the carpet mentality. Financial problems that are not solved by finding the source of the difficulty are doomed to continue until the root issue is resolved.

Just as anyone would push a pile from one side of the desk to the other America has continued a path of avoidance especially in regards to finance. The core difficulty of our national economy is that it is built on speculation. Just as any house or structure that is built on a faulty foundation is doomed to collapse, the same has happened to our economy. Until we fix the problem at the source we will experience repeated events of insolvency. The Fed has repeatedly bailed out banks and other financial entities that are deemed too big to fail. Referring to the bailout as economic stabilization gives the American people a new term that has a friendlier connotation, and will placate the general public with a more acceptable term for something they would otherwise be outraged. It is not unusual for government to designate policies or events to make them more readily digestible, such as referring to war as a police action or torture as enhanced interrogation.

    An economy built on speculation as ours is can be unstable. The whims of a few investors can set the trend of a mass selloff that will send the industrial averages spiraling towards yet another recession. Selloffs can lead to recession and recession can lead to depression, which will cause large banks to fail and bailouts will occur. Bailouts will be termed "economic stabilizations" to soften the grievous financial jurisprudence. The total of bailout funds ends up being a very large sum of money and it has to come from somewhere. The American taxpayers are footing the bill for large corporate bailouts, the same middle class American taxpayers on the verge of losing their homes and possessions without any chance of a bailout. The people who do not have enough to eat are paying for the corporate retreats some of these board of directors have given themselves with the hard-earned dollars the Fed gave them to keep their proverbial ships afloat. The really awful thing about this scenario is the greater percentage of the population does not know who paid for the mess to be cleaned up, and how it can affect them in the future. John Q. Citizen paid for Big Bank to stay afloat and with the trickle-down effect John Q. will continue to pay in irregular installments.

The latent effect for the Middle American consumer is when recession hits, the basic essential commodities that bolster our existence become more expensive and some unaffordable. Healthcare has to be considered a luxury in some homes, and with food costs escalating at an exorbitant rate many households are cutting back on fresher healthier items because they simply cannot afford them. Unfortunately for the American people they cannot elect someone who can fix these problems in one term. The probability of economic recovery in less than ten years is remote at best. An overhaul of our financial structure is required and the present government in place is not moving in that direction and not likely to be any time soon.

The super Pac backing that puts our leaders in office will not allow such changes to take place. As long as elected officials depend on campaign contributions to get them in office the public is doomed to walk the same path for as long as it takes to amend the election process. Until the election process has been rectified the financial changes, which are necessary to bring America back to some semblance of financial global leadership, will not occur.

The Government enforced no requirements on banks for dispersement of cash. The financial stipulations written into the original document, but later revisions were added because the banks threatened not to accept the money (Taibbi). Monies that had been originally earmarked for home lending and small business the Government reduced from their original intent to an insignificant amount. In theory the billions had been intended to help Middle America, but after a great deal of political maneuvering the end result was that big banks became bigger and if they had once been considered too big to fail, they became even bigger and created a more substantial safety net for themselves. The proverbial candy dish offered by big government and intended for homeowners and small business was snatched away by a bully of enormous size and financial hunger. Had the original restrictions been adhered to, this probably would not have taken place or at the very least not to the extent that occurred. Furthermore, if systems are in place and they are ineffective and or not enforced, what recourse do the American people have at this point, can the courts become involved after the fact to undo any financial injustices that need rectifying? If the American people were swindled out of seven hundred billion dollars that some percentage of which should have been distributed to the aid of small business and home lending, would the possibility exist that someone could say we want our money back, and if so could there be a reasonable course to retrieve said funds and reroute them to their original intended destination?

As rivers that flow into the sea become salt water, funds that become intertwined with big business grow tainted to the extent that they can never be fully recovered or returned to their pristine mountain stream state. With exploration of how bailout funds were dispersed and the discovery of certain irregularities therein attained, it would be reasonable to commence a recovery effort to reclaim monies from bonuses and corporate retreats in violation of the original bailout stipulations. Even if a small percentage was recovered it could be used to save a home or feed a child who might otherwise go hungry.

Turning back the clock has never been a viable option for financial misdeeds; as a gambler would relate, once the bet is lost it is gone forever. This has not been the case for large banks and other financial conglomerates. They have been given a third free throw, a fourth strike or a mythical second chance after overextending themselves and ill-advised lending. They gambled and lost, yet are given a second and more than likely third chance to speculate yet again. This would be acceptable if big business was playing the game with their money, contrary to John Q. Homeowner who if he were to gamble on a not so affordable mortgage and lose his job, there will be no Fed or any other financial entity to step in and pay off an ill-advised mortgage. If the average citizen revises his retirement stock portfolio to include higher risk and larger gain investments and loses his retirement, he will simply have to continue working.

The fact that our economy is built on speculation is the prime factor of our financial dilemmas. Factoring the loss of funds through too many layers of bureaucracy and simple mismanagement, our financial backbone has been systematically gambled away to the extent that financial recovery is seemingly impossible. Speculation in moderation is an acceptable form of financial gain. However, if speculation is the primary form of profit or as in the American case the cornerstone of our financial system, changes need to occur and rapidly in order to ensure some form of financial security for the future. As profits become harder to attain the more the tendency to speculate is utilized by corporate America. The desire for quick solutions is understandable, but the obvious pitfall of the nation when funds that do not really exist are gambled and lost. A gambler's thoughts are often described as innocuous musings and rationalizations to commence a dominance of the internal dialogue regarding when to quit and the irrepressible one more roll to recoup losses. National addiction to gambling is at an all-time high, and that is without factoring in speculative behaviors such as the stock market and short-sale real estate. It is no big mystery that our populace at all economic levels participates in games of chance, whether financial or otherwise. These behaviors manifest in a desire to attain wealth quickly. Sometimes that desire is born out of desperation because of debt, and sometimes originating from the inability to procure a level of financial comfort in reference to savings and retirement. The speculative nature of our national economy has a trickle-down effect from the Wall Street boardrooms to the living rooms of Middle America, where each entity will bet more than can be reasonably lost in an effort to better their respective financial situations. The main difference between the two being an errant boardroom decision that precludes billion dollar losses has a good chance of being underwritten by the Fed, because that boardroom entity is considered too big to fail.

The deceptive nature of those involved in the procuring and spending of the bailout funds cannot necessarily be deemed criminal, but the audacity in which it was achieved goes beyond measure. The original proposals for small business written into the verbiage to pacify doubters and essentially to sell the proposals to Congress were readily disposed of, not being deleted just simply ignored. So the good faith and intention that was the inspiration of the Home Affordable Modification Program (HAMP) act and its successors were subsequently purged from the active applications of the bailout and not to be mentioned again until more funds were sought. When original bailout proposals were being drafted there were objections by some that if there were too many restrictions the banks would not participate (Taibbi1). This could have been a turning point in this financial debacle, because financial institutions would not accept government money because of too many restrictions, then let the game continue without them, and provide the bailout money to those who are willing to participate within the prescribed guidelines. A wake up call was missed at that juncture, for if the same banks that would not participate because of conditions were more than likely the same who dealt out bonuses and funds for corporate retreats. Creating incendiary reaction by public and media in regards to the cavalier attitude in which the public funds being dispersed. This would not preface enlightenment that the authors or the first bailout would be once burned and twice warned. In the subsequent bailout maneuvers the recipients of federal funds used what was intended for economic simulation to pay off their previous TARP loans and what turned out to be a reduced interest rate. The American taxpayers were duped again, although indirectly as they were represented by the Fed and Congress. If financial conglomerates were subject to the same scrutiny and stipulations that a homeowner would have to face in initiating a new loan, one would find a great deal less irregularity in their financial behavior.

Legalities aside, the corporate bailout proved a travesty to the sanctity of American Jurisprudence, since the regulators assigned to oversee the giant nest egg were out sleuthed by the media. If overzealous media personnel did not actively investigate the whole TARP fiasco it's highly possible that a great deal of the improprieties that occurred would have gone unnoticed by the actual government personnel assigned to the task. If the federal government were left to its own devices many financial misdeeds would be swept under the carpet or better described as blown away from the immediate area as the landscaper's helper blows leaves from one yard to another.

It is criminal to allow funds to be diverted from their intended destination, to be invested in an ill-advised manner, and one must tread a fine line to follow the cash trail and then determine if legalities are infringed upon. Intent is a hard thing to prove and if the subject is a well-informed financial professional the burden of proof becomes even more taxing. It is an honorable thing to catch and prosecute individuals that tamper with enormous sums of cash, although once accomplished the cash is rarely recovered. Even if a conviction was attained it accomplishes little for the people that suffer the most, which are the lower income citizens who least could afford financial difficulties. It seems as though good intention by the president and Congress was thwarted by corporate moguls whose thirst for profits has driven them to erroneous investments that result in financial hard times for everyone but themselves.

When the large conglomerates fail the government will have to pay, regardless of whether a bailout occurs or have to subsidize thousands of workers who are suddenly without sustenance. The point of concern is whether the amount of cash can be monitored and directed to those who would most require the assistance. Essentially it would be ideal to have what human nature dictates, the innate behavior of helping beings in distress to be directed to feed the hungry not overload the coffers of the fabulously wealthy.

Confidence lost would be an accurate description of the bailout and its aftermath as the American people try to dig themselves out of a financial pit that was created when Congress allowed seven-hundred billion dollars to be entrusted to unscrupulous financial entities that did not use their windfall as prescribed.

Exhaustive research has revealed financial ramifications of not only the bailout of corporate America, but also the core problems that led to the downfall of some of our largest and seemingly indestructible financial institutions. The leanings of our government, however noble in their original ideas, are to fix problems in an easy manner rather than solve issues from their core which would be the most beneficial for the future. The continuance of these financial problem solving philosophies will only add to their complexity and also the longevity of their existence. If some semblance of restraint is achieved and a more critical thinking approach is adopted towards these financial endeavors there could be a chance for economic recovery. Leadership on all levels would have to work in unison to achieve financial recovery, as the political infighting is counterproductive to the process. The foibles of corporate America parallel a gardener blowing a mess of leaves to another yard rather than picking them up and mulching them, or at the very least just picking up the mess and moving on.

Work Consulted

Bernanke, Ben S. "A Cautiously Optimistic Economic Forecast." Vital Speeches Of The Day 76.1 (2010): 32-36. Academic Search Complete. Web. 11 Mar. 2013.

Bernanke, Ben S. "Bank Supervision In The United States." Vital Speeches Of The Day 73.2 (2007): 61. MAS Ultra - School Edition. Web. 11 Mar. 2013.

Bernanke, Chairman Ben S. "Flexibility And Optimism In An Unpredictable World." *Boston College Law Review* 50.(2009): 941. LexisNexis Academic: Law Reviews. Web. 11 Mar. 2013.

Fabian, Nelson. "MANAGING EDITOR's DESK. World Rankings Of The U.S. ... Education ... NEHA." *Journal Of Environmental Health* 73.7 (2011): 58-38. *Academic Search Complete*. Web. 7 Mar. 2013.

Heike, Jöns, and Hoyler Michael. "Global Geographies Of Higher Education: The Perspective Of World University Rankings." *Geoforum* (n.d.): *ScienceDirect*. Web. 7 Mar. 2013.

Kuhl, Lester. "maintaining a nation's middle class in the global economy: a systems engineering analysis of the american economic system and the middle class." *world future review* 4.2 (2012): 83-95. *academic search complete*. web. 7 mar. 2013.

Siskey, Kyle, and Elizabeth Fournier. "How The Bailouts Should Change Regulation." *International*

Financial Law Review 27.11 (2008): 20-24. Business Source Complete. Web. 10 Mar. 2013.

Taibbi, Matt. "Secrets And Lies Of The Bailout." Rolling Stone 1174 (2013): 34. MasterFILE Premier. Web. 16 Mar. 2013.

The Texas Decriminalization of Marijuana

Texas should pass legislation for the legalization of medical Marijuana. This legislation should accomplish several things. First the legalization of Medical Marijuana in Texas (lMMT) should provide increased tax revenue for the state government to help with budget constraints. Secondly the (lMMT) would help law enforcement with a reduction in drug violence statewide. Thirdly the (lMMT) would provide symptomatic relief to cancer and Aids patients who suffer from ailments that are relieved by medical Marijuana. Finally the (lMMT) would cause a de-valuation of Marijuana, and that will make it a less desirable product for illegal importers and organized crime syndicates.

This type of legislation has already been tried in several other states, including California, Colorado, and Alaska. It must be noted that the Federal government has made no concessions to the medical use of Marijuana and still considers it illegal. The technical legality between Federal and State governments presents a difficult situation for respective law enforcement agencies. Bostwick tell us "As an increasing number of states legalize marijuana's medical use, the federal government maintains its resolute stance that its use for any reason is criminal, a stance that renders prescribers simultaneously law-abiding healers and defiant scofflaws. (172)" State officials must adhere to State laws as written, and at any given time their policies can be over ridden by Federal officials. "Despite marijuana's current classification as a Schedule I agent under the federal Controlled Substances Act, a designation declaring it to have high abuse potential and no currently accepted medical use, physicians and the general public alike are in broad agreement that Cannabis sativa shows promise in combating diverse medical ills" (Bostwick 172). While States are allowing Botanical growers to produce Medical Marijuana, it is only at this point being allowed to continue while the Federal government turns a blind eye in that direction. The definition of Botanical growers in reference to Medical Marijuana is varied from state to state, but the essence is growers who produce medical Marijuana in a greenhouse environment and under strict control as far as the counting and registering of the plants on an each basis. This system creates an inventory control factor and the whereabouts of the product can be monitored to eliminate theft and misappropriation.

The decriminalization of Marijuana can be mitigating factor in the war on drugs. As the law enforcement officials can concentrate more on hard drugs such as heroin and methamphetamine which are more destructive to society and very addictive. The production of methamphetamine and heroin have increased in the U.S. over the last decade these type of addictive drugs have an effect that produces an increase in theft and robberies because the addicts will go to great lengths to procure their drugs. With more man-hours to work with because the police are not concentrating on Marijuana law enforcement and can be redistributed to eradicate hard drug crime.

"Nonetheless, many believe a lot less blood would be shed if America were to legalize pot, which according to some estimates accounts for 60 percent of Mexico's drug trade with the U.S., in much the same way that ending Prohibition in 1933 cut short the careers of tommy-gun-wielding gangsters. "(Conant, Eve et all 1) Legislation cannot generally eliminate crime, however if it can reduce drug related homicides it would certainly be worthwhile.

The concentration factor of medical Marijuana has thus far not been addressed in any current legislation. The concentration being the percentage of tetrahydrocannabinol (THC) present in the harvested form of the marijuana plant. This concentration affects the medicinal potency of marijuana as well as a contributing factor of the cash value of the crop.

Bostwick from the Mayo clinic tells us "Anyone with a credit card has ready access to blueprints for marijuana propagation and culture. The concentration of -9- tetrahydrocannabinol (THC), the psychoactive ingredient in cannabis, ranges from less than 0.2% in fiber-type hemp (so-called ditch weed) to 30% in the flower buds of highly hybridized sinsemilla." (173) this high percentage of THC is what botanical growers strive for in their pursuit of a higher grade product.

For the patient or consumer the larger percentage of THC will mean a smaller dosage, but the smaller dosage will also mean a more costly prescription. As devaluation of botanical Marijuana will occur from the legalization of medical Marijuana the prescription price will drop and unfortunately so will the profit for the grower." The fact is that many small time growers are paying their mortgage and feeding their families from profits on illegal marijuana. Nobody is going to vote to reduce the price of weed from $300/oz to $60/oz when that takes food out of their kids' mouths. (Vlahos, Kelley Beaucar 18) If law makers are looking to reduce the amount of Marijuana grown in the States they should consider legislation that will ultimately de-value the product and therefore disillusion the growers that produce the product.

However from the standpoint of what the state of Texas should do about this problem, it should be noted that the presence of drug markets in border areas, particularly in Juarez, and Brownsville have demonstrated a very abnormal murder rate. ", according to the FBI, more than 1,600 people were killed by cartel violence in Juárez. El Paso, a city of 755,000, recorded just 18 murders in the same year. Laredo had 11 (del Bosque, Melissa)" Quite simply if the emergence of Marijuana legislation could reduce the drug violence in the previously stated areas it certainly be worthwhile to proceed with the necessary litigation to implement these laws concerning botanical Marijuana in a timely fashion. What makes the drug trade attractive to organized crime is the high profit margin. If the profit margin were to be reduced and the involvement of organized crime factions along with it, the overall crime rates would be diminished accordingly. These factors alone would make the Marijuana legislation a worthwhile endeavor.

The prohibition description has been applied to Marijuana initiatives as an indication that laws do not necessarily prevent consumption of an illicit substance, but it has proven to be an enticement for organized crime to become involved in the process. The American consumption of

Marijuana has been a motivating factor to those individuals that cultivate and smuggle Marijuana."How does one win a drug war when millions of Americans who use recreational drugs are financing the cartels bribing, murdering, and beheading to win the war and keep self-indulgent Americans supplied with drugs?"(Conant, Eve, and Katie Maloney 1) If a large percentage of people are habitually using an illicit substance and the existing laws are not a deterrent, then the law as it stands is not having the desired effect. The existing Marijuana laws are not preventing the use of the drug, but creating criminals of individuals who would otherwise not be considered criminal. These laws are not designed to create criminals, but rather to prevent the consumption of controlled substances and prevent their distribution and sales.

One of the big problems legislators have with Marijuana is their theory that it is a stepping stone to more dangerous and addictive drugs. That ultimately the use of Marijuana will influence individuals to try other drugs such as Heroin, Cocaine, and Methamphetamine. This progression has certainly occurred, however there is no conclusive evidence to back up that claim."
According to Golub, Johnson, Dunlap, and Sifaneck (2004), drug surveillance programs have observed that marijuana use increased and the use of crack, cocaine, and heroin decreased among American adolescents and young adults during the 1990s."(Becca Walls 129) If studies have shown that Marijuana does not necessarily lead to the use of harder drugs that argument frequently used by legislators can no longer be considered viable. If our lawmakers have well considered that a great deal of their

arguments have flawed origins in their thesis statements, and those flaws are based in improbable conjecture, they would be morally obliged to withdraw their support of anti-Marijuana legislation. Even when opposing parties are presented with overwhelming evidence contrary to their established beliefs, they may not necessarily take any action to change their vote or publicly change their stance on an issue.

According to Vlahos, Kelley Beaucar the annual cash crop of California Marijuana could be worth in excess of fourteen billion dollars (18). If a state such as Texas could extract thirty percent from fourteen billion over a period of ten years and have that accumulated nest-egg of tax dollars to help with budget shortfalls and the improvement of education facilities the state would certainly have to give more critical thought and attention to the legislative changes. Money is not always a prime motivator, but very influential to constituents as well as lawmakers. If presented with a couple boxcars full of cash, that has been legally acquired and ready to spend, as incentive it would be difficult for lobbyists, legislators not to take a more serious inquiry into what had been considered an definitive negative answer. Hypothetical numbers aside any surplus revenue that could be acquired through Marijuana taxation would be a desirable event considering that revenue does not presently exist. The fact remains that a large percentage of Texas citizens are presently using Marijuana and are not deterred by current laws in that regard, and if tax revenue could be gained from that use it would certainly benefit the state of Texas.

This paper has attempted to explore and discuss the possibility of legalizing Marijuana in the state of Texas. A primary advantage of this type of legislation would be in a reduction of violent crime associated with the sale and importing of Marijuana. The de-criminalization of a controlled substance, historically as in the repeal of prohibition, has lessened the illegal activity formerly associated with that activity. The death toll in border areas where illicit drug trafficking occurs would be reduced.

The medicinal advantages of Marijuana for cancer and aids patients would be an improvement in the quality of life for nausea and lack of appetite sufferers. The medicinal qualities of botanical Marijuana have been documented in reference to their respective levels of (THC).

The de-criminalization of Marijuana would decrease the value of the plant from the perspective of consumer prices. If the Marijuana consumers are paying far less it stands to reason that as the profit margin falls so does the enticement of organized crime factions to continue to be involved in its sale and distribution.

In summation, if the aforementioned reasons for the legalization of medical Marijuana are to be noted as the reduction of violent crime associated with illicit drug sales, the benefit of Marijuana for medical applications, and the de-criminalization and ensuing freeing up law enforcement to move on to other more urgent tasks. It would be logical to assume that the legalization of medical Marijuana would be beneficial to the state of Texas. One could assume that if something is beneficial and logical that legislators would hurriedly put into effect any law that could reduce crime, help suffering individuals, and quite possibly help law enforcement. Overall this type of legislation would be a great benefit to the citizens of Texas and would hopefully be acted upon sometime in the near future.

Work Cited

Becca Walls, et al. "North Americans' Attitudes Toward Illegal Drugs." Journal Of Human Behavior In The Social Environment 19.2 (2009): 125-141. SocINDEX with Full Text. Web. 23 Oct. 2012.

Bostwick, J. Michael. "Blurred Boundaries: The Therapeutics And Politics Of Medical Marijuana." Mayo Clinic Proceedings 87.2 (2012): 172-186. Academic Search Complete. Web. 23 Oct. 2012.

Cockburn, Alexander. "Obama And Marijuana: A Great Betrayal?." Nation 294.25 (2012): 10. Academic Search Complete. Web. 22 Oct. 2012.

Conant, Eve, and Katie Maloney. "Pot And The Gop." *Newsweek* 156.18 (2010): 30-

35. *Academic Search Complete.* Web. 22 Oct. 2012.

del Bosque, Melissa. "Hyping The New Media Buzzword: 'Spillover' On The Border." NACLA Report On The Americas 42.4 (2009): 46. MasterFILE Premier. Web. 24 Oct. 2012.

Joffe, Alain, and W. Samuel Yancy. "Legalization Of Marijuana: Potential Impact On Youth." Pediatrics 113.6 (2004): e632-e638. Academic Search Complete. Web. 23 Oct. 2012.

Martin Finkel, et al. "Decriminalization Of Cannabis - Potential Risks For Children?." Acta Paediatrica 100.4 (2011): 618-619. Academic Search Complete. Web. 23 Oct. 2012.

New Analysis Of Marijuana Incarceration Data: "Who's Really In Prison For Marijuana" De-Bunks Common

Myths Advanced By Drug Legalization Advocates. Rockville, Maryland, US: White House, Executive Office of the President, Office of National Drug Control Policy (ONDCP), 2005. PsycEXTRA. Web. 23 Oct. 2012.

Feral Hogs Surf Asphalt

The celebrated running of the Hogs on the nation's fastest freeway, on the grassy slopes alongside IH one thirty just outside Austin Texas, lives a population of feral hogs some of which are descended from Russian boars and other boutique swine. These collective swine are lined up to surf the mechanized wave of autobahn vehicles, like Malibu locals waiting for their perfect set of waves. The IH one thirty recently proclaimed the nation's fastest freeway with a speed limit of eighty-five. Bear in mind most drivers take a poetic license with speed limits to presume eight to twelve miles an hour over the posted speed limit as the accepted margin. To set the scene we have three and a half ton vehicles traveling ninety five or more miles an hour and two to four hundred pound hogs running out

into traffic with imminent collisions about to occur. According to the nearest sheriff's department, drivers should not swerve to avoid contact with the hogs, but go ahead and let the collision happen and hope for the best. The sheriff's claim that too many drivers swerve to avoid the hogs and end up in a rollover accident with sometimes fatal results. One would not need a physics lesson to know that a high-speed collision with a large animal and a crumple sensitive sports car is a catastrophic event. If a nine-pound goose can bring down an F-14 then a two hundred pound hog will surely end the journey of a beamer.

The question comes to mind, why are these pigs out here don't they have a farm to go home to, aren't there spiders for them to converse with, is asphalt cold fusion bacon really their future. The reality is these pigs

are lost souls. Their plight of homelessness and being hunted by men in helicopters, when those helicopters aren't too busy ferrying wealthy tourists to Grand Prix races, is one of nomadic wanderings along what is the closest thing to an Autobahn that exists in the U.S... These swine are displaced for various reasons; some wealthy industrialist wants to create a wild game ranch for weekend fun and then imports some Russian Blue boars and other exotics and then his hedge fund evaporates and the exotic animals are left to fend for themselves, others are crossbreeds from farms and ranches that need fences mended and others that are simply wild to begin with.

According to Wildlife Biologist Rick Taylor "There are currently an estimated one million feral hogs in Texas." These hogs are considered a nuisance wildlife

population and are not protected by hunting restrictions by seasonality. They are a danger to small or young livestock such as infant goats or lambs. Their main destruction factor is to agricultural environments by rooting and spoilage of crops by random foraging. Feral hogs can multiply quickly with litters from three to twelve pups and a gestation period of three months from females able to bear at six months of age. (Taylor 5) Although there has been a perennial bounty on these animals little has been done to reduce their current population, due to their natural speed of reproduction.

To examine the supposed thought process of a feral hog, do they see headlights as an enticement to run into what might be a sunrise or an intruder of sorts into the realm of their domain? It might be that there is little or no rational thought to their behavior, and that their

running out into traffic is actually innate behavior to an unknown light source. Mal intent is certainly not in the capabilities of swine; although they are a displaced and hunted population their limited thought process excludes them from deviant behavior.

There was rumor some months ago of a bacon shortage. There might be a probable solution to two different dilemmas. The quality and taste of the flesh of these animals as long as it is carefully prepared is considered by many to be a delicacy. The probability of reducing the population of feral hogs utilizing current methods is unrealistic; however the possibility of examining and innovating methods to market and produce feral hog products is realistic. Instead of hunting and disposing of the feral pigs, with a little fencing and a bit of surplus grain the population could be nurtured and

then harvested to supplant any shortage of pork bellies. With revenues derived from the sale of Interstate wild bacon a budget could be created to launch a wildlife conservatory habitat where feral populations of the future could be protected.

Feral Hogs Surf Asphalt

The celebrated running of the Hogs on the nation's fastest freeway, on the grassy slopes alongside IH one thirty just outside Austin Texas, lives a population of feral hogs some of which are descended from Russian boars and other boutique swine. These collective swine are lined up to surf the mechanized wave of autobahn vehicles, like Malibu locals waiting for their perfect set of waves. The IH one thirty recently proclaimed the nation's fastest freeway with a speed limit of eighty-five. Bear in mind most drivers take a poetic license with speed limits to presume eight to twelve miles an hour over the posted speed limit as the accepted margin. To set the scene we have three and a half ton vehicles traveling ninety five or more miles an hour and two to four hundred pound hogs running out

into traffic with imminent collisions about to occur. According to the nearest sheriff's department, drivers should not swerve to avoid contact with the hogs, but go ahead and let the collision happen and hope for the best. The sheriff's claim that too many drivers swerve to avoid the hogs and end up in a rollover accident with sometimes fatal results. One would not need a physics lesson to know that a high-speed collision with a large animal and a crumple sensitive sports car is a catastrophic event. If a nine-pound goose can bring down an F-14 then a two hundred pound hog will surely end the journey of a beamer.

The question comes to mind, why are these pigs out here don't they have a farm to go home to, aren't there spiders for them to converse with, is asphalt cold fusion bacon really their future. The reality is these pigs

are lost souls. Their plight of homelessness and being hunted by men in helicopters, when those helicopters aren't too busy ferrying wealthy tourists to Grand Prix races, is one of nomadic wanderings along what is the closest thing to an Autobahn that exists in the U.S... These swine are displaced for various reasons; some wealthy industrialist wants to create a wild game ranch for weekend fun and then imports some Russian Blue boars and other exotics and then his hedge fund evaporates and the exotic animals are left to fend for themselves, others are crossbreeds from farms and ranches that need fences mended and others that are simply wild to begin with.

According to Wildlife Biologist Rick Taylor "There are currently an estimated one million feral hogs in Texas." These hogs are considered a nuisance wildlife

population and are not protected by hunting restrictions by seasonality. They are a danger to small or young livestock such as infant goats or lambs. Their main destruction factor is to agricultural environments by rooting and spoilage of crops by random foraging. Feral hogs can multiply quickly with litters from three to twelve pups and a gestation period of three months from females able to bear at six months of age. (Taylor 5) Although there has been a perennial bounty on these animals little has been done to reduce their current population, due to their natural speed of reproduction.

To examine the supposed thought process of a feral hog, do they see headlights as an enticement to run into what might be a sunrise or an intruder of sorts into the realm of their domain? It might be that there is little or no rational thought to their behavior, and that their

running out into traffic is actually innate behavior to an unknown light source. Mal intent is certainly not in the capabilities of swine; although they are a displaced and hunted population their limited thought process excludes them from deviant behavior.

There was rumor some months ago of a bacon shortage. There might be a probable solution to two different dilemmas. The quality and taste of the flesh of these animals as long as it is carefully prepared is considered by many to be a delicacy. The probability of reducing the population of feral hogs utilizing current methods is unrealistic; however the possibility of examining and innovating methods to market and produce feral hog products is realistic. Instead of hunting and disposing of the feral pigs, with a little fencing and a bit of surplus grain the population could be nurtured and

then harvested to supplant any shortage of pork bellies. With revenues derived from the sale of Interstate wild bacon a budget could be created to launch a wildlife conservatory habitat where feral populations of the future could be protected.

Music Downloading and Effects on the Music Industry

This paper will explore the effect of music downloading on the music industry. To define music downloading briefly as the illegal downloading of recorded digitized music from sources that does not represent or contribute monetarily to the artists from which the music originated. Although there are legitimate websites that sell digitized recordings, they do not represent illegal activity. This work will concentrate on examining entities such as Napster which was at the forefront of the illegal music downloading movement. Napster presented an argument that their format could bolster music sales by exposing many varieties of music that consumers would not normally hear.

(Farshid Navissi Vic Naiker Stewart Upson 167)

However music industry executives claim Napster's responsibility for loss revenue would far out weigh any advantages gained by varietal exposure of different genres of music. With the development of ITunes by Apple in 2003, the music industry had a source of legitimate sales from which to draw revenue from digitized music. Changes to the music industry would be brought on by the digital advancements of recording and processing. Hereafter the tour budgets and promotional activities would be greatly reduced and the golden age of recording would be a thing of the past. The excessive revenue driven activities and subsequent profit margins would be curtailed by the emergence of Internet oriented musical products.

    Napster's inception was before any Digital Rights Management (DRM) was enabled. The Internet was wide open and there were no precedents for the governing and policing of digitized music and related items. An entity such as Napster could not be held legally accountable for taking advantage of an opportunity to make a profit where the law had no restriction, although a moral quandary should have them consider the rights of the artists that were not being compensated for their work. There came a flood of Internet consumers that was tailor made for Napster and other internet music sharing providers. These modern internet consumers had little regard for the profit margins of large record companies. The modern young digital music enthusiasts took full advantage of the wide open internet, and built huge libraries of sounds and musical works valued beyond measure to themselves, but highly valuable in lost revenue to the record companies. These types of downloads have changed the music industry tremendously. Daryl J. Woolley from the University of Idaho indicates some astonishing figures regarding downloading:" The total cost of pirating music is estimated at $12.5 billion annually, of which $5 billion is a direct cost to the recording industry."(31)

W. Jonathon Cardi relates in a 2007 article from the *Iowa Law Review* "The public proved so hungry for online music that over sixty million Americans turned to a life of crime by way of copyright infringement in order to get their digital fix."(836) the loss of revenues to the music industry has had a vast trickle-down effect. Even roadies and guitar technicians had a 60% reduction in wages when budgets started to dwindle according to George Benson's guitar technichan John Mooy on a recent interview on youtube via the *SeymourDuncanChannel.* Mooy also stated that crew members would have to assume more work behaviors than previously expected. In essence the guitar technicians would have to double and sometimes triple their respective workloads by taking on the responsibilities of individuals who had been eliminated by budget constraints. The large budgets were gone and the types of tours and promotions that had been prevalent would be severely altered. Music corporations would have to restructure their marketing, promotions and Artist relations. The wine and dine era has come and gone with smaller overall gross revenue to work with the record labels will have to rethink their complete infrastructure.

The value of a song by the public perception has become a topic for discussion.

Even if a single song on ITunes costs 99cents it has perceived value below that price. Sandulli and Martin-Barrero relate "that the current price for digital music, on average 99 cents whether dollar or euro, is considered too high by P2P users."(4) If the consumer is unwilling or unmotivated to purchase music at a perceived value that is less than its acceptable market value. Then consumers will be further inclined to download their music rather than purchase it. If market strategies remain where they are the profits will continue to decline and profits will severely decline. The ensuing changes and development of the music industry will be driven by their ability to adjust as the technology dictates.

Digital Rights Management (DRM) has become a necessary guidance factor in the new music industry. Copyright infringement and digital music ownership have become intertwined with the other problematic facets of profitability in the new music industry. "The economic status of music changes once it can be separated from the tangible object."(Birgitte Andersen · Marion Frenz 716) Changes for the music industry have come from dealing with what was once a physical product to an intangible entity that has value but no physical presence. Although the digitized music product has what could be considered a onetime production cost the relative cost of recording is the same. The post production costs that include manufacturing of disks, tapes, and vinyl records are virtually eliminated. Therefore the profit margin should increase without the post production costs, however with the reduction of overall sales this has not been the case.

A somewhat unsuccessful method of preventing downloading was file pollution.

"In order to fight P2P piracy, the recording industry decided to deposit into file sharing networks large volumes of polluted music files."(Sandulli-Martin-Barrero5) These polluted files could include white noise, random distortion, and sound level fluctuations. Sound quality could be differentiated from standard versions by overly compressing or limiting the song selections to create undesirable listening experience. "From a theoretical point of view, pollution reduces significantly the quality of reproduction of the songs, limiting the degree of substitution between the legal song and the illegal one" (Sandulli-Martin-Barrero5) In an industry that is highly dependent on satisfaction of their consumers, the pollution of musical files could be considered a highly improbable proposition, if consumers were to mistakenly receive the polluted musical files. The pollution methods were a considerable deterrent and will continue until better technological methods arise.

The criminalization of individuals who download digitized music, most of whom are minors, has not filled our jails or prisons. Unfortunately the public perception of the illegal music downloading is likened to the taking of soap or towels from hotels, in that it is technically stealing but considered by the general populace to be socially acceptable. These types of illegal activities have not been easy to enforce or gain convictions. Chien-Yi Huang of National Taipei University relates in a recent article "Piracy is the greatest threat facing the global music industry today. Because of the widespread domestic use of high-speed broadband Internet over the past decade, consumers can easily reach, copy from, and upload music to the Internet."(1) However the music industry strives to continue to criminalize and label the offenders as pirates and Internet thieves.

A great percentage of music downloaders are college students age 18-24. In studies done concerning this age group it has been noted that this group has a general dissatisfaction with the music industry as a whole. This peer group has a general perception that the record companies have too large a profit margin. Their beliefs and opinions influence their collective behavior towards downloading and digitized music piracy.

> Several studies indicate that many individuals,
> particularly young college students, are unsatisfied

> with the current price of music and. Indeed, the price of music and its implications for the consumer are relevant to students' decisions to download music for free For example, found that concerns about price were among the strongest predictors of future intentions to illegally download music, even among students who had never done so before. In addition, found a moderate correlation between beliefs that CD's were not worth the high price record companies charged and previous downloading behaviors. **(Jambon** et all 1)

If their collective belief is that the downloading behavior is not really a criminal act, and record companies have a surplus of profits, then the college students behavior is not really hurting anyone. In summation, the Music industry has been severely altered by the influx of digitized music downloading. The overall profits have been reduced and all aspects of the business have been changed. Budgets for touring musicians have been greatly reduced and the methods for how those tours have been scheduled, and conducted have also been changed. The trimming of spending has caused technicians, sound engineers and other behind the scenes individuals to double up on their respective workloads. The physical changes of the industry, such as no longer having a physical product to manufacture, reproduce and package has created what seems like a better profit margin. However it has been shown that the diminished sales due to music downloading have outweighed any financial gains from reduced production costs.

More Artists can be exposed to the public via the Internet. Music aficionados are able to scan vast websites of choices of musical artists from all over the globe. This gives them an exposure not previously possible before the advent of digitized music. Theoretically, the increase in exposure would help increase sales of songs on the internet,

but the typical digitized music consumer has been shown to illegally download rather than purchase especially when their original search was conducted over the Web. The record companies continue to market their digitized product in hopes of swaying the balance against Internet downloading.

Record company executives also are trying to educate prime market groups about the criminalization of music downloading and software piracy. The overall effects of digitized music piracy have been a serious financial burden to the music industry. The subsequent reduction of revenue has been a financial burden to artists, executives, songwriters and al related individuals in the music industry. Profits have been greatly weakened and budgets for tours, artist's development, and production in general. The music industry has been crippled by the insurgence of digitized music downloading.

Work Cited

Andersen, Birgitte, and Marion Frenz. "Don'T Blame The P2P File-Sharers: The Impact Of Free Music Downloads On The Purchase Of Music Cds In Canada." *Journal Of Evolutionary Economics* 20.5 (2010): 715-740. *Business Source Complete*.

Bourreau, Marc. "A Comment On Peitz And Waelbroeck." *Cesifo Economic Studies* 51.2/3 (2005): 429-433. *SocINDEX with Full Text*. Web. 23 Sept. 2012.

Cardi, W. Jonathan. "Über-Middleman: Reshaping The Broken Landscape Of Music Copyright." *Iowa Law*

Review 92.3 (2007): 835-890. *Academic Search Complete*. Web. 23 Sept. 2012.

Chiou, Jyh-Shen, Hsiao-I Cheng, and Chien-Yi Huang. "The Effects Of Artist Adoration And Perceived Risk Of Getting Caught On Attitude And Intention To Pirate Music In The United States And Taiwan." *Ethics And Behavior* 21.3 (2011): 182-196. *Philosopher's Index*. Web. 23 Sept. 2012.

Navissi, Farshid, Vic Naiker, and Stewart Upson. "Securities Price Effects Of Napster-Related Events." *Journal Of Accounting, Auditing & Finance* 20.2 (2005): 167-183. *Business Source Complete*. Web. 23 Sept. 2012.

Sandulli, Francesco D., and Samuel Martín-Barbero. "99 Cents Per Song: A Fair Price For Digital Music? The Effects Of Music Industry Strategies To Raise The Willingness To Pay By P2P Users." *Journal Of Website*

Promotion 2.3/4 (2006): 3-15. *Communication & Mass Media Complete*. Web. 23 Sept. 2012.

Rocky Mountain High

The spark of freedom has our nation inhaling a legal Rocky Mountain High.

If Colorado and Washington State can get away with defying the federal government by legalizing marijuana for recreational use, it will set an incredible precedent. Colorado recently passed legislation to legalize marijuana in a recreational form for adults over the age of twenty-one, and in doing so symbolically challenges the federal government to make an objection or forever hold their peace. If states are allowed to pass legislation in direct conflict with federal laws, there will be an unbelievable floodgate opened for new and creative legislation. Were Texas to abolish federal income tax within its borders would Washington DC be inclined to look the other way? States should be allowed to self-govern to a certain extent; however the line that is drawn in the sand has certainly has been crossed by Colorado and Washington State by their recent Marijuana legislation.

It remains to be seen if Drug Enforcement Agency agents will parachute from the sky in a massive statewide raid, exclaiming "hands up citizens if you can see us through the smoke and drug-induced haze you now dwell in". The DEA would be within their rights and jurisdiction to attempt such a raid. The problem for the DEA would be, do they have enough manpower, and if their ranks are lacking, perhaps they can recruit from the nation's unemployed. Our country has a lot of individuals without jobs and healthcare. These recent events concerning drug laws could provide a solution for the nation's economy. Newly deputized DEA agents could have decent paying employment as well as the renowned federal employees' healthcare package. As long as they do not partake in newly legalized Marijuana usage they can stay in good standing with their new Federal employers and possibly be eligible for a favorable retirement package.

If other states were to follow suit and create legislation that was to conflict with existing federal laws and statutes, therein lies a possibility for a nationwide domino effect. The balance of power between the states and the federal government would be completely torn asunder. In order for the federal government to enforce any edicts or directives they would have to recruit more and more individuals to be employed in a massive deployment of unprecedented magnitude in order to staunch the national wound of unrest. On a positive note, a vast recruitment would put a great deal of people to work who currently only utilize their prehensile digits for remote control use, and these new hires would be paying taxes and spending their newly surplus incomes on commodities that would hopefully arouse and stimulate our national economy.

If large raids occurred and vast amounts of marijuana were to be seized, the seized material would have to be catalogued and hopefully put to good use. The medicinal quality components could be reserved for patients who require its healing and nausea-relieving effects. The larger branches and trunk-like material could be utilized for the making of ropes, paper and uniforms for our burgeoning DEA population's training manuals, uniforms and macramé inspired-restraining manacles. Hemp paper products could also be used for official documents and anti-drug propaganda pamphlets.

Our government has had a history of making good use of seized materials, and in our current economy it would serve us well to be as frugal as possible.

To make the best of a bad situation has been, or used to be the American way. When danger was near we strengthened our borders or took decisive measures. Now in the face of impending civil unrest due to the collision of state and federal legalities, we must quickly seek a logical and value-driven solution to this legal dilemma. Will it be an unprecedented federal mandate that forces States to repeal legislation that clearly violates federal law? If this type of forced repeal were to occur it would forever change the relationship between states and the federal government. This type of resolution should certainly be avoided if at all possible, because the political fallout would be catastrophic to an already economically weakened nation. In a perfect world the Federal government could lend some legal experts to help states examine possible ways to amend or rescind recent legislation that although liberal and logical in spirit, clearly is more problematic in its implementation and clearly illegal by federal law. In conclusion let us not mar our nation's purple mountain's majesty with a drug induced and legalistic haze.

In the Shadow of Mount Shasta

We wandered through the crisp mountain air towards the horse barn in anticipation of a snowbound trek in the shadow of Mount Shasta. It was not just that you could see your breath; there was also a unique flavor to the air. The flavor of pine and juniper was in the air along with a certain freshness that might bring to mind mint or cinnamon, but in the background of the palate, a subliminal sense response to high altitude atmosphere that has body as well as flavor. Great clouds of exhaled air accompany each step in the frigid mountain air, and each step has its own signature squeak as I tread across the crisp powdery snow. The roofs of the barn and ranch house are completely blanketed with snow and the ground is a white fluffy carpet as far as the eye can see. In the distance the tree line of Silver tipped pines completes a landscape that is dominated by Mount Shasta. In my youth I had seen the silhouette on soda cans and although a familiar shape the aluminum imagery fails miserably in comparison to the majesty of the view that one can behold so close to the ethereal entity. The ancient Indians of the area revered the mountain as a source of creation, and modern cultists believe Shasta to be a point of significant harmonic convergence. There is no doubt of the impressive visage of the view and the wispy crown of stratus clouds adds to the Olympian portrait.

    Uncle Jake got one of his hands to saddle a horse for me, being able to ride fairly well, but still enough of a greenhorn to not be trusted to equip the horse for a winters ride in the snow. There was only one horse available and Jake's niece who was my host acquiesced the mount to me. For the sake of poor recollection I will refer to the mount as Shadowfax, as he was capable of galloping through the snow without any visible effort or fatigue. After I had mounted the steed I felt as though I was a character in a surreal film or even a figure in a popular cigarette commercial romping in the frozen tundra with great clouds of exhalations from Shadowfax and myself in a stoic demeanor. I was almost dressed for the part having denim jeans and a North Country wool shirt with a down vest, but alas no Stetson or Winchester to complete the ensemble. I trotted and galloped for as long as I was allowed within the confines of the ranch's fences and brought Shadowfax back to the barn feeling as though I had conquered all of Northern California and Middle Earth as well. The ride was over and the elapsed time escapes me, although the memory stayed vivid for decades.

What could possibly complete a morning such as what I have just described one might ask. With a reasonably short drive through the picturesque mountain country and unequaled vistas along the route home we arrive at our destination. The mountain home of our temporary residence, with its roaring fire place that magically heats the whole house with an ingenious system of furrows in the slab foundation, that disperse heat from the fireplace to all rooms within the house. The instant the front door is opened the warmth beckons you inside, and the smells from the ample kitchen heighten my already voracious appetite. My eyes as well as other senses drank in platters of fried eggs that still have wafts of steam rising from them and the scent of bacon, along with other platters of hash browns and country bacon. Toast already slathered with high grade butter piled high enough to not be dwarfed by the other dishes on the table. A pitcher of fresh squeezed orange juice blushed with cranberry and a pot of prequel Seattle coffee complete the menu. People often speak of a New England or country breakfast as their ideal morning meal; these would pale in comparison to the Northern California breakfast that I had that day. I am not sure how much I ate and have very little memory of the conversation that accompanied the meal. Suffice to say that comfort does not just reside in the cushions of a chair, but in the feelings that come from an exquisite meal and the aftermath of an adventurous morning outing that fulfills the spirit and the intrinsic warmth that comes from a mountain hearth.

Snow day

I am watching the ticker on the bottom of the screen for closings of schools and roads, and low and behold there it is the messiahic message, Eanes is closed and so is Bee Caves road thereby creating the much coveted snow day. I jump up and almost spill my morning dark-roast brew, and proceed to do a touchdown dance somewhere between Chuck Berry's duck-walk and MJ's moonwalk, all without any permanent injury. As soon as the kids found out that school was cancelled, their former sleepy demeanor vanished and they became almost uncontrollably enthusiastic. Snow days rarely occur in Austin, Texas, when they do it seems the thing to do is go outside and embrace the ice and snow, especially if you have children. The year of this photograph escapes me, but the feeling of winters chill and families sharing of Nordic delights has endured the test of time. We dared to dwell under the ice-cycles for a photo opportunity and ended up with a great picture. My daughter had reached her peak height, while my son a full head and shoulders shorter than myself, is almost that much taller than me now, some many years later.

    I get the kids and myself as bundled- up as possible and prepare to head out into the frozen wasteland that our yard has become. Parkas, hats, and gloves the seldom used items of warmth are miraculously found. I don my chocolate colored cowboy hat. A hat if you wear for a certain period of time in freezing weather, you can joyfully take off quickly, and watch a miniature steam cloud arise from your head. Sadly on this occasion we were not able to capture this phenomenon. It is surprising how warm a beaver hat can be. I don't want to be considered "all hat no cattle" by my contemporaries, but the warmth provided by such headgear is worth any criticism from neighbors from other parts of the country.

The air has a different aroma when the temperature falls below a certain range. The cedars seem to permeate the air better around the freezing zone. The invigorating scent of winter is a special treat to the senses. When you walk on a slightly frozen lawn there's a delicious crunch that you cannot hear often enough.

On this particular day there wasn't enough snow to make a snowman. We improvised by making an ice sculpture, thereby ruing my L.L. Bean deerskin gloves I had been carting around since my Boston days. We gathered ice-cycles and other random shards of ice and created a structure similar to Superman's controls in his underground lair. The ice that had formed on the patio table created a large circle to make triangular pieces that the kids enjoyed breaking into decorative shapes. The process was every bit as stimulating as building a snowman, but much more artistic. We took a few pictures and came inside to thaw. The post-thaw feeling of throbbing hands and faces can be eased by copious amounts of hot chocolate laced with marshmallows.

Part of the thrill of a snow day is spending quality time with your children, and the iced-in factor lends a sense of adventure to the situation that would not otherwise be present on a regular day-off. There is also a certain joyful feeling that arises from the spontaneity of an unscheduled day of artic leisure.

Children have a special smile for these types of occasions. It is a smile that cannot be duplicated by television or random rodeo clowns. The type of joy Dani and Jean had on this particular day cannot be re-created or planned regardless of parental imagination.

I don't recall seeing a clock that day. I know that at some point it got dark and soon thereafter we had dinner, which tasted especially great due to the winters celebration. Then we drifted off to a winter's nap of epic proportions.

When we awoke the ice sculpture was greatly altered, and that sculpture was the only remaining ice in the yard.

American Human Trafficking

A nationwide epidemic in human trafficking continues unchecked, despite some efforts by legislators to combat the fast spreading problem. Whether the victims are from the U.S. or foreign countries we need to do everything possible to alleviate the issue. The primary reason for trafficking is the sex trade, but there are many instances of domestic or agricultural labor abuses as well. The efforts to stop the victims from entering the country at border stops are not effective. The police can help when they are made aware of situations, but victims are not always ready to report these crimes due to various reasons. Legislation, such as the Trafficking Victims Protection Act of 2000(TVPA) have demonstrated promising ideals; however their implementation has yielded little success. Further versions of TVPA have shown theoretical improvement and created a field of awareness that did not previously exist. The moral dilemma for U.S. citizens to consider is the reason that the underage trafficked sex trade is rampant here, is because as long as the appetite for this trade exists someone will endeavor to provide the product. There must be a responsible effort to re-educate our population regarding the nuances of the problem and the treatment of those afflicted with deviant sexual appetites.

By definition trafficking is described by Allison Cross from the McGeorge Law Review as "the recruitment, harboring, transportation, provision, or obtaining of a person for labor or services, through the use of force, fraud, or coercion for the purpose of subjection to involuntary servitude, peonage, debt bondage, or slavery."(400) The steps taken to refine and describe the verbiage associated with human trafficking has made the job easier for legislators to begin the task of creating viable laws to combat the rising epidemic. Awareness is essential to creating a successful arena to undertake an active approach to eradicate the human trafficking problem.

The ability of police personnel to recognize victims is essential to prevent dual victimization. Dual victimization exists when human trafficking victims are arrested and prosecuted as prostitutes when their abusers have forced or coerced them to commit illegal sexual acts thereby creating a duality. If the victims are treated as such rather than being treated as criminals and able to be recognized as potential witnesses against their abusers they may have a chance at reentry into normal society.

When victims are prosecuted and then released into their former situation the cycle of abuse continues. The problem exists that a great deal of these victims refuses to testify against their abusers. This sometimes occurs because the victim is emotionally involved with their abuser and even in some cases married or related and or adopted, making them unable to differentiate between the assumed loyalty and their own basic rights as free individuals. It has also been observed that many individuals are coerced by threats to family that is not present, but controlled in former residences that their abusers have access to and some hold over. The reality of the extent of the control that some of these abusers have over their victims is shocking to believe, and in some instances unbreakable. The battle would be easier if the police always had the complete cooperation of victims in their attempts to obtain convictions.

The interpretation of prosecution laws are also a factor in the war against human trafficking. If the police are arresting a much greater number of alleged prostitutes and thereby giving an illusion that law enforcement is soft on prostitution consumers. It stands to reason that the consumers are less likely to restrict their deviant sexual behaviors if the penalties are not enforced with the same fortitude as the prosecution of prostitutes regardless of age or trafficking status. Tessa Dysart provides FBI data as follows; "According to the FBI's 2010 Uniform Crime Reports, for jurisdictions that provided information on the sex of those arrested for prostitution and commercialized vice, 68.7 percent of those arrested were females, making it likely that the prostituted person was arrested more often than the buyer."(637) There is a problem inhibiting the successful battle with human traffickers, because there is a conflict of duties where officers have too many tasks that concern possible detainees and prostitutes. From Professor of the Harvard Law Review; "the same persons charged with protecting [victims] are also charged with deporting undocumented persons, arresting prostitutes, and detaining and charging those working without authorization."*(1013)* Subsequent versions of TVPA in first reauthorization in 2003 and then again in 2005 and an additional version backed by President Bush in 2006 which directly addressed domestic minor sex trafficking. For all the criticism George Busch received during his presidency he strongly advocated this bill and demonstrated empathy for the victims it was to protect. The William Wilberforce TVPA of 2008 further strengthened the act by adding provisions for the training of relevant officers to recognize victims of human trafficking and prevent wrongful prosecution and the creation of juvenile residential treatment facilities for the rehabilitation and re-indoctrination into society of victims. Further provisions of TVPA 2008 were the creation of laws with stiffer penalties for offenders who traffic in underage children and the provisions for forfeitures of asset gained in the related criminal activity. Provisions were also created to provide civil remedies and restitution for victims and the designation of sex offender for those who traffic children.

Conflicting laws between federal and state governments present a unique set of circumstances regarding the prosecution of minors in sex crimes. The federal law states that a minor cannot be charged with prostitution because under federal law a minor prostitute is designated as a sex trafficking victim. However, in many states minor sex trafficking victims have been charged with prostitution and convicted. "In 2010, according to the FBI's Uniform Crime Reports, 804 minors were arrested for prostitution and commercialized vice, including 91 persons under the age of fifteen. Of this number, 656 were females, including 69 girls under the age of fifteen."(632 Dyssart) The Columbia Human Rights Law Review statistics provide a good example of state and federal inconsistencies regarding minor sex trafficking victims (MSTV) and an inability to identify minor sex trafficking victims at the state level. The success at the state level relies on better training of police, prosecutors, social service providers and judges in their treatment of MSTV. Additionally the inconsistency of state minor sex trafficking laws can lead to a migratory procession of traffickers to states with more lenient laws. "According to a NCMEC estimate, 10,000 prostitutes were brought to the 2010 Super Bowl in Miami. Indiana, fearful of a similar situation when it hosted the 2012 Super Bowl, passed a more stringent state trafficking law."(633 Dyssart) Although the problem of state versus federal governments regarding MSTV can become transitory, the real moral issue remains that there is an overzealous appetite for the minor sex trade and the vacationers or sports enthusiasts that are away from home and have an insatiable desire for something that defies all religious and moral codes and ethical behaviors. Yet the real criminals in this issue continue to perpetuate the problem and until they have been re-educated or rehabilitated or received psychiatric treatment to prevent further deviant behavior the MSTV problem will be ongoing.

The child sex trade is big business. According to Dyle of McGeorge Law review; "The Commercial sexual exploitation of children is big business. Sadly, today there is no better return on money than selling a child for sex. The International Labour Office estimates that human trafficking generates at least $32 billion annually" this fact displays the alarming trend of legal leniency towards consumers and perpetuates the cycle of MSTV's. Legal penalties are being raised and conviction rates are still very low. Legislation is taking care of business in regards to tougher stance on MSTV, but enforcement and prosecution are still lagging behind.

Identification of victims is the key element in successful processing of MSTVs. Once they are in what should be called protective custody, they must be allowed to sense an element of trust from enforcement officials. The beginning of mutual trust and comprehension will hopefully enable officials to gather intelligence and strategies to prohibit a return to abusive environments and the possibility of gathering testimonial evidence which would increase the conviction rate. One of the biggest drawbacks to increasing conviction rates is the inability to secure successful testimonial evidence from MSTVs. This inability could be because MSTVs have an inordinate amount of misplaced loyalties to their abusers. Sometimes the loyalties are due to relationships based on co-dependence or illusionary romance brought on by perpetrators intentional psychological conditioning and even drug dependency and subsequent staged withdrawal.

As in any high profit business the strategies are not accidental and the recruitment processes are dictated by consumer demand. The demand has steadily increased over the last decade the methods of the perpetrators have become more sophisticated and the people at the top of the food chain have continued to further insulate themselves from the lower levels thereby securing there longevity in their criminal endeavors.

The proprietors of the sex trade are motivated by greed and the highest dollar transactions frequently are associated with underage subjects. While this fact does not stem from any logical human condition or psychological abnormality it makes it hard to define and identify the consumers of the underage sex trade. They are not all obvious sexual deviants that are reminiscent of novel characters we are all so familiar with. A great deal of these sexual deviants are our neighbors and sometimes even family or friends. We fail to recognize the hidden behaviors and sometimes intermittent activities of these people because they are our friends, neighbors and family, and are not necessarily subject to a great deal of scrutiny towards deviant sexual behavior. These types of sexual desires are not unique to metropolitan environments and could be equally prevalent in urban and rural areas as well. The rehabilitation of these deviants is essential to the successful reduction of the MSTV dilemma. The identification and subsequent processing, conviction and rehabilitation of these criminals can only be achieved by careful and diligent police and other law enforcement individuals If possible when MSTVs are apprehended a DNA trail can be created to identify any person or persons that have relations with the victim. In order to establish this type of trail the DNA database would have to include sex offenders and those possible offenders that had previously plea bargained their conviction to lesser charges. In the event that former sex offenders are paroled and rehabilitated their DNA profile will always be in a sex crimes database that could be continually updated to include viable suspects as well. As science progresses the eventuality of an international database of DNA signatures secured at birth will create an unmistakable trail to the violators of underage children and young adults. These prospective methods will invariably cause uproar in human rights violations and will also create a moral dilemma in regards to violation of someone's personal privacy against the protection of MSTVs and other related crime victims.

The eventuality of further legislation to follow the progression of TVPA bills and the development of State's whom have also created bills to protect MSTVs in their respective Sates the Human Trafficking problem will hopefully be reduced and kept somewhat in check. Although human trafficking is a nationwide problem and addressing the issue by pointed legislation is admirable, the root of the problem is the deviant sexual appetite of parts of our population, and until this aspect has been addressed the legislation will only accomplish keeping politician's legislative records looking good for their constituents. The deterrents created by later versions of TVPA are commendable in their proactive clauses that can label offenders as sex offenders and the asset confiscation aspect would hopefully intimidate the intended criminal element. However, unfortunately the targeted criminal element is rarely in the proverbial sights of our law enforcement officials. The upper echelon of the sex trade crime lords have thoroughly insulated themselves from the business end of the criminal activity, and have also erased the monetary trail that would tie them to any illegal activity. The federal law definition of child prostitution as trafficking is a commendable attribute to recent legislation and if the State governments would adhere to this definition the frequency of MSTVs being prosecuted for crimes that the Federal government has stipulated as victimization rather than prostitution, there would be a chance for more rehabilitation and placements in social service facilities. The accurate and decisive identification of

MSTVs and sexual deviants in their respective rolls will have a more positive effect on the MSTV problem by eliminating unnecessary prosecutions and facilitating the successful convictions and subsequent rehabilitations of sexual deviant offenders.

Americans need to take a close examination of existing deviant behaviors in our society and their long term effects on the youth of our country. If the influential and governing entities of America turn a blind eye to these types of problems and continue to ignore the issues that chip away at the foundation of our society. It is the moral responsibility of every American to concern themselves with the protection and safety of our younger population. This responsibility includes a dedicated sense of diligent awareness towards moral issues concerning American youth and their educational and moral development without and deviance or criminal encumbrances related to MSTV and related issues.

Santa Cruz

It was a foggy morning in Santa Cruz, but of course when was it not foggy in a northern California beach town in the morning. There was a fog in the air and a fog in our heads. The previous night's revel had lasted late into the night and you could hear the foghorns from the bay. Evidently the seamen were early risers and blew their horns without any respect for our foggy and swollen heads. The smell of the sea mixed with the scent of the local fauna was familiar from many previous visits to Santa Cruz. Manzanita and Pine along with a mix of other trees made for an interesting scent unique to Santa Cruz.

We were staying at my friend's parent's beach house and it was spring break. Nine or more high school students crammed into the house bunkhouse style. It was one of many beach houses that were of various associations. Some were summer houses of the parents of people we knew, and others such as my aunts, were family places that did not usually welcome or tolerate spring breakers.

My fellow revelers were still sleeping and it was a good time for a walk on the beach. Most of the aforementioned houses were actually on the beach, except for the one where we stayed on that particular trip. So it was more than a few strides to get to the beach. Once on the beach I headed toward the boardwalk, walking on the waterline where the sand is a little firm and the scent of the sea is mixed with the fragrance of seaweed that has accumulated during the night. The morning is a great time at the beach. The crowds are not around and the usual noise factor was gone. The solitude of a walk on the beach at sunrise was uplifting in a strange sort of way. The problems that are usually pondered seem a little less daunting when you are strolling on the sand. The rhythm of the waves was therapeutic. Decisions that were being debated within one's mind, such as, what to do about college were less threatening.

The view of the mountain range that surrounds the area became readily apparent when the fog started to lift. The coastal range frames the beach with panoramic belt of evergreen foliage. The Santa Cruz Mountains stretch from just south of San Francisco to the north and to the Pajaro

River to the south. The area is incredibly fertile and some of the finest wine grapes were grown there. What had begun as a mission town had blossomed into a popular beach resort that included California's oldest boardwalk.

It was time to turn around and head back to the beach house. Someone would have been awake to go out to breakfast. Although the beach house was fully equipped I do not remember anyone ever cooking anything there. The family that owned the house was once the largest beef producing family in the western United States, and it seemed that a barbecue grill would have been almost required, but there was none. Once back at the house I found a couple awakened compatriots to accompany me to Luther's. Luther's was one of those unique breakfast places that every small town should have. It was a very small diner style restaurant that puts out reasonable priced food with simple dignity for a nominal charge. There were no table tents advertising products that could be construed as promotional. There was no canned music, just a simple diner with excellent food that usually arrived quickly. Eggs over-easy and hash-browns and toast, along with some crude oil coffee and the day was ready to begin. The resumption of the revelry would have begun sometime after breakfast.

My associates for spring break were all from the local private Catholic school in our home town. We had been working together at a construction site, which oddly enough was owned by one of their classmate's father. One the day when we collectively asked off for the block of time for spring break we were collectively fired. So leaving our future in the construction business behind us, we began our sojourn to the coast from the flatlands of the San Joaquin valley. We packed the necessities that did not include food and commenced the epic journey. The drive from the center of the San Joaquin valley to Santa Cruz takes a little over three hours or the ninth loop of a Van Morrison eight-track cassette. I know this to be true because on another beach mission we listened to Moondance the entire trip, and had it been any other music album of lesser quality I might not have survived. Finally we arrived at our destination and unpacked our gear and surprisingly enough, we did not open windows and fluff pillows as most people do when opening a rarely occupied dwelling. Instead we stowed away our beverages in the fridge and headed almost immediately for the beach. It was a ten minute walk to the beach and another ten to the boardwalk.

    Even though we were a brotherhood of sorts we sought companionship of the sisterhood variety. Some of which that we met were from our town, but a different high school. It seemed strange that we would meet a group that was only five miles from where we lived, but they were nice girls and the three sisters from their group were very unique. The sisters were brunettes with sky blue eyes and dimples that would make you laugh. They seemed to collectively possess a sense of self that defied embarrassment. A definite grasp of living in the moment that was utterly charming, they seemed to like spending time with us and we kept in touch for a while after we returned home.

There is a myth about California beaches. Part of the myth is that people can swim and surf comfortably in the ocean. This a bit of propaganda more than likely created by the film industry at the request of the tourist bureau. The water is very cold and the further out you go the colder it is. I remember swimming in Santa Cruz in the summer and having my feet ache because of the cold. When you view footage of people surfing in California without a wetsuit it probably was filmed elsewhere or the actors were getting extra pay for their suffering. Although the water is very cold it smells of Abalone and Pine. It also tastes of minerals other than salt, whether this because of unreported oil or chemical spills is anyone's guess.

    The texture of the sand is different from other beaches. The sand seemed a touch finer than other beaches. There were no Dunes, but the sand extended quite a bit up the width of the shore. Just a few feet from the water line it was difficult to run, and there were just enough crustacean shells intermingled with the sand to keep your feet wary. The lifeguard towers were spread every hundred yards or so, and they were approximately eight feet high. The height is etched in my memory because I jumped off the top of one and thought I had ruined my knee. As it turned out it was only a light sprain and an easy payment for a reckless act of youth.

The Pier at Santa Cruz is old and creaky. It also possesses a great view of the area. There are shops and restaurants, bait shops, and interesting people to watch. The Pier also smells of dead fish, French fries and oily wood. It also smelled as though someone failed to make it to the restroom in time. It may have been that people were frustrate by the lack of personal facilities and were careless with their waste water. The Pier was a great place for fishing and crabbing. We mostly were crabbers. It was probably because all we needed was some string and bait, where fishing required more equipment than we could muster. On one occasion when we were crabbing we saw an errant pelican crash into a post. This seemed very strange because in general pelicans seem to be very good flyers and quite dexterous in their fishing and stunt-like aerial abilities. So we were almost speechless when the pelican hit the post. The bird did not pierce the post with its bill as one might expect, but slammed the telephone-like post, fell to the ground and flopped around for a minute and then walked off in a zigzag fashion. We looked at each other with the unspoken question of whether or not the event we witnessed had really happened. We left the Pier that day with a different opinion of Pelicans and of course no crabs.

    The celebratory bonfire was a matter of great excitement. There was no careful planning or safety procedures. We simply gathered enough dry driftwood to build a fire and dug a makeshift pit in which to house the fire somewhat responsibly. We were aware that too big a fire would attract undesirable attention from the local police, with whom we sought as little contact as possible. There was always a little too much damp wood in the fire and this made for a smoky side to the fire. So I tried to keep ahead of the smoke, but it seemed to follow me around the fire almost as though the smoke was stalking me. The conversation around the fire seemed to follow no particular course or direction, and the participants would speak louder and louder without listening to each other. The fire would always include songs from "American Graffiti" with a loose waiver for the semblance of pitch and meter. Enthusiasm would trump talent at the bonfire and there was an illusion that volume would enhance quality.

The Santa Cruz Boardwalk was an iconic amusement area. It had a wood framed rollercoaster and actual wood framed pier to accompany it. An overhead tram that ran the length of the Boardwalk was a great way to relax and get a great view of the area. The mixture of aromas was varied between the smell of the salt air with the scent of cotton candy, popcorn, diesel, and the sweet smell of countless sodas spilled by the patrons of the Boardwalk. The arcades with the destined to lose games, along with the more infamous rides such as the bumper cars and the Roundup were more popular with our group. The Roundup was a circular ride with strap-in sections along the interior of the circle. When the ride began it would spin at a fast rate and then slowly tilt till it reached ninety degrees of its axis. As the axis was reached the wind coming in off the ocean would rock the structure slightly terrorizing the riders by the unexpected aspect of the ride. It felt as though the whirling circle was being ripped from its mountings by the wind and I remember screaming to the attendant to stop the Roundup. Countless attendees had probably screamed to stop this ride or another and my plea was unanswered.

Trips to Santa Cruz were always special. Unfortunately, how special they were was not as readily apparent at the time. In the mindset of youth one did not always take the time to cherish the moment, or drink in the smells of trees, salt air or take a mental picture of the surroundings for later examination. We lived for the moment, and did at times appreciate where we were despite the fast

living appetites and behaviors of our existence.

Santa Cruz was the paradise we chose.

Santa Cruz Harmonic Convergence

There is a cell of very creative luthiers in Santa Cruz California, a veritable nest of tonal geniuses all working in the approximately the same geographical location in the production of fine acoustic and electric guitars, ukuleles, and similar instruments. The instruments they produce are unique in their appearance as well as their tonal signature. If a certain location can produce the inspiration for superior design and construction of fine guitars and their similar counterparts, then Santa Cruz has achieved that status. The exchange of ideas and sometimes exclusively essential equipment and ensuing results is similar to the Socratic era of Greek city States in its creative and inspirational environment.

Richard Hoover of Santa Cruz Guitar Company (SCGC) is one of the earliest builders of guitars in the Santa Cruz area. His acclaimed instruments have graced stages and studios all over the world. SCGC, created in 1976, has produced excellent guitars and also, through its apprentice program, acclaimed luthiers. Scott Walker, of Scott Walker Electric Guitars, started as an apprentice at SCGC after graduating from Roberto Venn Scholl of Luthiery in Phoenix, Arizona. Another renowned luthier in the area is Rick Turner of Renaissance Guitar and former founding partner in Alembic Guitars that was made famous by Jerry Garcia, Steven Stills and other artists. Turner is also well known for his innovations and developments of signal processing within guitars and his creation of pickups that produce a more realistic and cleaner sound for acoustic and electric guitars.

    Turner's Model-one which Lindsay Buckingham of Fleetwood Mac made iconic by his endorsement and continued usage on stage during touring. Model-one shares the tonal qualities of a stellar acoustic with the searing tones of a vintage electric without any of the feedback concern associated with stage acoustics in large concert and stadium venues. The switching of guitars during verses and choruses of songs was eliminated for Buckingham by the creation of the Model-one, because of the guitars ability to change from acoustic to electric tone by controls at a finger's touch on the guitar itself, thereby eliminating the necessity and distraction of guitar technicians racing on and off stage during the course of a song. The tonal clarity and ease of switching coupled with the unique style of Buckingham's playing made the Model-one a creative success. Turner's creation of the Renaissance guitar stage acoustic with zero feedback and concert quality sound was another example of his intuitive ability to re-engineer the signal processing and manufacturing process to build an affordable stage acoustic that sounded and played like one's favorite dreadnought without the usual concerns of large venue amplification. Turner's creation of the Compass Rose acoustic guitar with a flying buttress system of bracing, graphite rods, and innovative neck attachment design that aids in the deployment of tonally selected woods that reduce weight and heighten sustain and frequency range.

Rick moved to Santa Cruz in 1997 partly because he had begun to outgrow his shop in Topanga Canyon and also because he wanted to raise his child in a different atmosphere. The child's godfather, British musician Martin Simpson who was a Santa Cruz resident, suggested that Rick and family relocate to Santa Cruz. Along with the urging of luthier Richard Hoover from SCGC, the Turners left Topanga Canyon for Santa Cruz without regrets. Turner now works out of a 3500 sq. foot facility and produces twenty-five instruments a month. Turner enjoys the interaction with other local luthiers and, as he states, the occasional "careful restoration of unique instruments". In a recent interview Turner states, "I do enjoy working with special woods" and further relates the story of a Giant Sequoia that had fallen on UC Santa Cruz land in 1968 and was in embattled litigation for many years due to it being a forbidden to harvest status, and he stated, "it was 283' high and 27' in diameter and over 2700 years old, the wood was very fine grained and very deep red, and quite resonant." He described the wood as someone else might describe a rare wine or a forgotten Rembrandt, with a quietly stated reverence and enthusiasm. He further related that he had built "several ukuleles and three Model-ones" with a tone of respect for the unique elements and creations. Turner still performs with a band called the"Uke

Ellingtons" with a style that the name made obvious. Even after a long, storied career in the creation of fine instruments, Turner still keeps his talented hands in the day-to-day operation and only employs four other craftsmen in the production team.

Richard Hoover is the creator and owner of SCGC. He has been building guitars and training master luthiers for many years. His expertise in guitar building is almost unparalleled. If he did not reside or work in Santa Cruz there would be no one close to his ability in close proximity. Hoover has sustainability awareness for the products that he uses. He states in a virtual tour of the SCGC facility," the problem with irresponsible harvesting that removes a tree from an ecosystem, it also affects the livelihood of the local inhabitants" Hoover also related," we would not be part of deforestation." Hoover has a dedicated awareness to the path from forest to purveyor to luthier, and primarily utilizes reclaimed wood from reliable sources.

    Hoover has an extended knowledge of not only modern luthiery, but also the practices of Italian master violin makers. The ancient violin makers had a vision of extended the value of an instrument by building with an awareness of future generations that would be playing an instrument, and taking precautions in construction that would not only extend the life of the instrument, but also ease the probability of restoration by employing natural glues and construction methods that would facilitate the likely restoration endeavors. Hoover's tonal creation applications include hand tapping every piece of wood to analyze its tonal range and modifying the build to ensure the best tonal application. Hoover has compared the mass production methods of robotic engineering the wood to create guitar kits to" throwing rocks at a piano with your eyes closed… eventually you might hit a chord." Hoover knows what a guitar that SCGC builds will sound like before it is completed. Even though no two guitars will sound alike, he will have a very good idea as to what the tonal range, frequency range, and the type of sustain the guitar will exhibit. SCGC's adherence to responsible harvesting along with its dedication to producing the best instrument possible makes them one of the premier luthiers in the world, not just Santa Cruz.

Scott Walker began his own guitar shop after apprenticing at SCGC. He knew from the beginning that he did not want to build "three hundred dollar guitars." Walker knew he wanted to build ultimate guitars. Guitars with the widest frequency range, the longest sustain and an effortless playability, guitar characteristics that had been ingrained through countless conversations with artists, and also with his own personal experience as a guitar player. As shop foreman at SCGC, Scott oversaw a great deal of custom work, interfaced with top guitar players, and learned what they were seeking in their instruments. With the care and scrutiny of all hand-built parts, Scott currently turns out twenty-five instruments a year. When asked about the interaction between Santa Cruz luthiers, Walker described the results as "cross pollination". These luthiers are artists and, as such, they are not constantly looking over each other's shoulders; however, there is a great deal of sharing of ideas and sometimes equipment. Walker sometimes takes his guitars to Turner's shop to use his specialty sprayer. A great deal of modern luthiers utilizes nitro-cellulose for finishing their guitars. It is an organic compound that is plant-based and possesses a better tonal response than urethane, which is more commonly used in high production guitar making. Walker's use of Turner's sprayer is evident of a desire to facilitate the best and most efficient method of finishing his instruments. There is a lot of handwork in the creation of fine guitars and these luthiers Walker, Turner, and Hoover; fabricate their own jigs and other specialized tools for the work in their respective shops. An inherent enthusiasm for the materials and the designs they employ makes these luthiers unique. They are artists. The creations they fabricate could easily hang in museums or be mounted in hermetically sealed glass cases. Instead, each creation is almost a living being. The wood breathes. With the right handling, the guitar can sing. They are also immortal. In the right environment, a guitar could last an eternity; if treated properly a guitar can survive multiple generations and provide a unique voice for each respective generation. A guitar will slowly alter in sound quality as it ages. The timbre of the guitar's voice will mellow with age, and as it ages the guitar will sustain longer to a certain extent. When builders such as Walker approach a new project they are seeking the utmost for the customer; and conversely, the modern boutique buyer has high expectations for the premium price that is required. Guitars in the five- thousand and up range are a small market share; however, the buyers of these instruments are patient for the build which might take as many as six months to a year, yet they are also very critical in appearance, performance, and tonality of the product they receive. Buyers that put down fifteen hundred dollars to get on the production list, then an additional fifteen hundred to begin the project, and then pay the balance prior to shipping, expect everything to be perfect on arrival.

Kenny Hill is another Santa Cruz luthier. Hill's specialty is classic guitars. His evolution in guitar building includes a stint in Pachaco, Mexico where he studied with Mexican masters for eight years. Hill has developed a double top method that utilizes wood layers of wood with a layer of Nomex in between; this process enhances the projection ability of the guitar. Hill has also pioneered a venture to build guitars in China that are more affordable than his hand-built signature series, but not the lower quality associated with Chinese mass production. Hill's signature guitars are uniquely patterned after classic guitar builders Hauser, Torres, and Fleta. These assimilations have been painstakingly created after studying drawings of an 1836 Hauser that was a favorite of Segovia. An excerpt from an article written by Hill explains his thoughts on the double top method he employs.

I constructed the soundboard using two thin layers of wood separated by a layer of a honeycomb material called Nomex, but then I used a pretty conservative bracing system. What the heck, maybe I could get the best of both worlds. But then we come to the first question. When you go to a restaurant, the first question is, "Do you want ice water?" With classical guitars, the first question is, "Spruce or cedar?" Well, it's both. That's a cool thing with the laminated soundboard: finally I could use both spruce and cedar so I didn't have to ask that question anymore. But of course now I have to ask "Is the spruce on the outside or the inside?"(Hill)

Hill also related a story about a customer that was not getting the frequency response from his vintage 1937 Hauser.

> Speaking of ears, a guy in Southern California bought one of my '37 Hauser models through a dealer. I started getting e-mails saying "What can I do about the highs? It doesn't have any highs." And I thought "If any guitar has highs, that thing does." He lived eight hours away, but he didn't want to ship it. He said he would make the trip up and bring the guitar to me. Then I didn't hear from him for a while. One day an e-mail popped up. It said, "You might remember me. I was complaining about my Hauser with the bad highs. I went to the doctor and he pulled a 2" plug of wax out

of my ear. Now can you make any suggestions for a change in strings? The thing sounds too bright. (Hill)"

Hill has been published numerous times in various publications and has also taught at University of California at Santa Cruz. He splits his time between the boutique shop in Santa Cruz, the management of the plant in China, and teaching guitar-making classes. Hill's unique perspective is that he builds hand-made classical guitars that take a year to finish as opposed to the partnership in China that turns out guitars in a matter of weeks.

The luthiers of Santa Cruz create unique instruments that are tonally diversified and visually stunning. Richard Hoover best described the custom guitar building process as," complementary materials and a dedicated group." It would not seem to be a coincidence those creative minds and hands gravitate to a unique and idyllic location, such as Santa Cruz, to conduct their business of fine instrument crafting. Their respective instruments produce a harmonic convergence of a different magnitude, and un-paralleled by known regions. Their convergence on the area could be accidental, but the quality of the harmonics their respective instruments produce certainly is not. Their interaction, although not regimented is an enhancement to their creativity. Walker describes the interaction as "cross pollination", and Hoover calls it "symbiosis", but however it is labeled, the interaction is a contributing factor to their respective success.

The author had spent summers, spring breaks, and adult vacations in the Santa Cruz area. The fascination and rapture for the natural beauty of the area has been exceeded by the knowledge of the underlying creative force of the inhabitants. The successes of the Santa Cruz luthiers are the tip of the proverbial iceberg in relation to the mass of local artisans, writers, and academics that reside there. It will hopefully not be long before the writer again visits Santa Cruz.

Stockton beach

The water looked like a maelstrom of micro rainbows and arced splashes,

and yet there were patches of open water, still and shinning like glass.

Visions of celestial hail storms with crimson sashes.

The scent of lilac permeates the salty air.

Oceans transcend into rivers that refract the sky with cloudy patches.

A hum of voices eclipses the silence.

Light penetrates the mirror surface with prismatic rods and crystal lashes.

These visions of buried thought are apparent to those without despair